GIVE ME LIBERTY OR GIVE ME DEATH

GIVE ME LIBERTY OR GIVE ME DEATH

◆

Learn to live without cigarettes

Christopher A. Chausse

iUniverse, Inc.
New York Lincoln Shanghai

GIVE ME LIBERTY OR GIVE ME DEATH
Learn to live without cigarettes

Copyright © 2006 by Christopher A. Chausse

All rights reserved. No part of this book may be used or reproduced by any means, graphic, electronic, or mechanical, including photocopying, recording, taping or by any information storage retrieval system without the written permission of the publisher except in the case of brief quotations embodied in critical articles and reviews.

iUniverse books may be ordered through booksellers or by contacting:

iUniverse
2021 Pine Lake Road, Suite 100
Lincoln, NE 68512
www.iuniverse.com
1-800-Authors (1-800-288-4677)

ISBN-13: 978-0-595-38099-2 (pbk)
ISBN-13: 978-0-595-82466-3 (ebk)
ISBN-10: 0-595-38099-9 (pbk)
ISBN-10: 0-595-82466-8 (ebk)

Printed in the United States of America

Contents

Introduction ix

Part I   The Truth

Chapter 1   The Game 3
Chapter 2   A Dying Breed 8
Chapter 3   The Product 12
Chapter 4   Scrupulous Advertising 17

Part II   The Memories

Chapter 5   Learn to move on 25
Chapter 6   Beware of experts 29
Chapter 7   The sweet nectar of victory 32
Chapter 8   What's your take? 36

Part III   The Support

Chapter 9   Only the strong survive 41
Chapter 10   The pen is mightier than the sword 44
Chapter 11   Wind for those sails 49
Chapter 12   The Spiritual Side 51

Part IV The Divorce

Chapter 13 The dissolution 57
Chapter 14 Onward and upward 60
Chapter 15 The right directions 64
Chapter 16 Just a little odd. 67

Part V Staying Single

Chapter 17 Maintain your distance. 73
Chapter 18 What's in it for me? 76
Chapter 19 Take the high road. 79
Chapter 20 Finally, let's clear the air. 82

Part VI (TCM) Time Compartment Management

Chapter 21 How TCM works 91
Chapter 22 The Final Countdown 128

In Closing 133

1 Corinthians 13:13 Now these three remain: faith, hope, and love. But the greatest of these is love.

Introduction

On March 23, 1775, to conclude his timeless speech, Patrick Henry uttered these words: *"I know not what course others may take; but as for me, give me liberty or give me death!"* His speech was eloquent, but delivered with passion, and was an attempt to motivate the Virginia Provincial Convention to bear arms against the British, and fight to the death if necessary to protect liberty and guarantee the freedom for Virginians, and all Americans. And although the freedom of thousands of lives is not on the line here, your own personal freedom is; and it's time to fight for your liberty, your freedom from cigarettes. As an ex-smoker, I can testify to one thing: When that "give me liberty or give me death" attitude instills itself in your heart; when you know in your gut that victory is certain, you'll quit. It's that 'the point of no return' and when you get there, nothing will stop you, and I mean nothing. Will it be hard? Sure it will. It'll be tough as hell, but it won't matter, and I'm going to try to help you get to that point if you're not already there. And yes, as the title indicates, I believe that smoking is a learned habit, and I also believe that to stop smoking, you only have to learn how to, and is just a process.

Whether the inspiration to quit smoking comes through divine intervention, a warning from a doctor, your child pleading with you, your spouse begging you or maybe something just changed in your minds eye, take advantage of it. For many smokers, such as myself, it takes a long time to get to that point. However for a select few, something just clicks and it's an overnight decision. Either way, no matter which one of these groups you're in, it's vital that you start working on it immediately. The reason is that there is a small window of opportunity, filling the spirit with hope, which frees up the mind and allows the heart to believe in the possibility that maybe, just maybe you can do it. Unfortunately, far too many smokers just dismiss the thought of quitting smoking. I mean hey, it's hard to quit right? And I know that from experience because I've quit numerous times before finally being successful. I believe that you're looking right through that window of hope at this very moment…please don't let it go.

Fact or fiction

This was the title that I read on a quit smoking course: "Stop smoking in one hour!" Do you believe that? I don't. Here's another one: "You can stop smoking even if you don't want to." Are you kidding me? And there's another one that says, "Easily quit smoking in 24 hours." Well, guess what? There is no easy way to quit smoking. And as far as that one-hour thing…I don't believe it for a minute! There's no easy way to break an emotional, chemical and psychological habit that you have solidified over the course of 5, 10 or up to 30 or 40 years, at least not permanently. Quitting cigarettes sucks and is absolutely no fun at all, but is so worth it. The real question is this: "Why do you want to quit?" If you can figure out the *why*, that's all you need, then I can help you with the *how*. Here's a statement from a 27-year smoker: "If you know the *why*, the *how* will effortlessly follow." Oh I've heard all the negative people that demand, "I know the why, tell me the how!" Well, there are thousands of volumes of information on the how and most of it is free. Unfortunately, these negative people are the same people that seem to forget that it still takes something called *effort!* The only problem is that the *why* hasn't transformed into a *need* yet.

In my humble opinion it only takes one solid thought in your mind to succeed at quitting smoking, and here's the formula: *Make is a need rather than a want.* How? That's your job to figure out…and nobody else can do it for you. Think about this for a moment: If your doctor said that if you didn't quit immediately, you probably wouldn't live more than another 6 months, I mean quit right now, would you make it a need then? Of course you would, so then, what would it take for you to make this a need rather than a want? Answer this question and you found your reason, and all you need is one reason…just one.

I doesn't matter what kind of personality you have, be assured that someone has quit smoking and succeeded that was far worse off than you. It's a decision, a mindset, and that resolve gets stronger with time for those that succeed. I'll say that again: *The resolve gets stronger with time for those that succeed.* I will not paint a false fairy tale picture because the process is nerve racking, but the end result is like no other victory that you have ever known. In my life, very few things compare with the feeling of finally being free from cigarettes.

Identical differences

No two smokers are alike and because of that, there really isn't any one specific way to succeed at quitting cigarettes. I heard once that the only "one way" is the way that works. Amen to that! Here's an analogy: I've done a lot of research concerning the legendary Martial Arts Master and Philosopher Bruce Lee, and how he preached his style of Martial Art, which is called Jeet Kun Do. If you're not familiar with him that's okay, but just understand that he was supposedly never beaten in empty hand combat in his 32 years on this earth. I've read much about this amazing man and his philosophy was very simple, which was this: There should be no form or style. The only style is to have no specific style; the only form is to be formless. People that learned this Martial Art were taught according to his or her own strengths and weaknesses. The student's strengths were exploited while the weaknesses were absorbed into the strengths over time through the process of self-development, meditation and study, only to eventually to become the new strengths. One example of this: Just like Bruce Lee mastered the art of high kicks, few know that he, prior to coming to America, never kicked above the knee. So his weakness eventually became is strength, and his trademark. So tell me then, why shouldn't we practice that same philosophy when quitting smoking? That's why I'm opposed to "canned" quit smoking programs. Understand that what works for me will, more than likely, not work for you. However, you can probably extract many useful things from how I did it, my philosophy if you will, possibly some of my views, ideas and techniques from my experience, and then apply them to your own personal program tailored for you…by you. What a concept.

I have a very simple system that I will share with you that helped me quit the cigarette habit successfully and permanently after 27 years. Much like the analogy from the above paragraph, you do it your way, and all I do is point you in the general direction with a little advice and maybe a nudge to get started.

You never know

You may never pass this way again so please don't take this lightly. This is your future we're talking about here. This could very well be the most important task of your life, and one that affects the lives of those close to you, those that love you dearly. Now, I have only one request: Take what you need from this book, and throw the rest in the trash. What I mean is if you don't like page 23, just rip it out and throw it in the trash, but be accountable to yourself and have the commitment to see this through. And remember: *Nothing worth doing is ever easy, but it is always worth it.*

PART I
The Truth

1

The Game

The Rules

It seems to be a game to them. They spend more and more money on luring in new players every year, the smoking public that is. Smokers keep dying by the thousands or worse; live in misery for a few years before the inevitable finally happens. Our kids keep starting (most before age 18), the government stays supportive but of course it's all within the letter of the law, and they keep making billions....yes billions.

This isn't like most games though. This game is different for only one reason, there is only one winner...them. They're doing everything they can to keep their loyal customers. The truth is this: Of consenting adults in 1974, 44% of them smoked; and in 2004 it's only 21%. We're getting there but have a ways to go yet. Our kids, well, they think they look cool because they have a cancer stick in their hand. Or maybe they feel older and more mature. And as for the adults that have already been smoking for 20 years, well we know that 70%–80% of them say they want to quit but far too many lack the confidence that they can beat the habit. It's not a game anymore; it's just wrong.

Here are some interesting facts about a very large tobacco company named Phillip Morris USA that will make you doubt their "fair play." Here's what they do plain and simple: They make cancer sticks, cigarettes, fags or whatever name you wish to call them. Regardless of what their website says, they're part of the problem. Here's what their website has to say, and I quote:

> Philip Morris USA's (PM USA) core business is manufacturing and marketing the best quality tobacco products to adults who use them. Our brands include Marlboro, Virginia Slims, Benson & Hedges, Merit, Parliament, Alpine, Basic, Cambridge, Bristol, Bucks, Chesterfield, Collector's Choice, Commander, English Ovals, Lark, L&M, Players and Saratoga.

Here's the translation of what we just read in above paragraph:

"Let me introduce myself: I'm a multi-billion company that makes a product that contributes to the death of hundreds of thousands every year and promotes countless sicknesses. If you're curious, here's the list of my weapons that I've been killing you with for years. You and your families have been loyal over the years so I paid a fortune for some well versed legal representative to come in here and write the verbiage for this killer (pun intended) website. He keeps it politically correct to the letter, which keeps the government from fining me a few hundred thousand dollars for bending the rules, not that I couldn't afford it anyhow."

Okay, am I making you think a little? Wait, here's more of what I read on their site, and again, I quote:

> At Philip Morris USA (PM USA), we demonstrate our commitment to responsibly marketing our products to adult smokers by developing and implementing programs that comply with both the letter and the spirit of the laws, rules, policies and agreements that govern our business practices.

I don't believe they made themselves clear. Here's a translation:

"I found some loopholes in the Tobacco Settlement Agreement of 1998. I also needed some help with the wording on my site, as well as our advertising, so by paid a couple advertising agencies a million dollars or so, which I can afford, thanks in no small part to your loyalty, and I got the best money could buy. Of course I promised not to advertise to children so instead; I'll increase my marketing budget by about $8–$10 billion annually to accommodate for this little offset, so my profits shouldn't suffer at all. And since our pesky government is restricting how I can spend my millions on advertising, I'm going to have to add some chemicals to the tobacco to make them more addictive so my loyal customers will be even more addicted thereby giving them even less of a chance to quit the habit that has made us so darn successful. This will make up for the dip in sales due that annoying agreement little we had to sign. By the way, if you want to ever quit smoking, but we hope that you won't, we support this wonderful quit smoking program. Please click on the link below."

Okay, I know what the actual text was but this has to be the most controversial site that I've ever seen in my life. They're sitting on the fence by saying, in not so many words: We're sticking by the law, we're making billions, oh yeah, just so the government doesn't give us a hard time, we endorse this quit smoking program too (see I told you we cared about our customers). Am I the only one that gets furious over this crap? No matter what the laws or restrictions, they have their ways of bending the rules to their advantage because it's all about the money baby!

Furthermore, the tobacco industry as a whole pays millions of dollars to several organizations to keep the smoking public from believing they can quit. They do this by paying some moron with a PHD to write a report that only states half the truth. The million dollars that they pay these 'experts' is a drop in the bucket when you're making tens of billions of dollars a year.

True Lies

Now I do understand that they're selling a product that people buy voluntarily, but I also believe in fair play. If you want to make tiny holes in the filters of cigarettes to lower the readouts on the toxin reports, tell them you're doing it. And don't hide behind that cheap circus trick and say that you're making it healthier to smoke…give me a break! There are articles published by the United States Government that state that nicotine is as or more addictive than heroine and cocaine. Here's my question: Should we, the American public, believe this when all you do is deceive us in every area other of this subject, and numerous others? Should we believe you when the fact is, you're probably paying some professor from the 'University of Deceit' a few hundred thousand dollars to help you sell this line of crap to the American public? And just because he has some credentials from some college, then we're supposed to believe it, right? Wrong! Be your own expert and know the truth because it's out there. I will not assume that an industry or our government to a certain point, which promotes this self destructive habit to the tune of tens of billions of dollars a year, gives a crap about me or any other person. It's a nasty game they're playing and they have the money to endorse whatever they want, whenever they want for whatever price they choose. I'm not trying to badmouth our government but I also know that there's a lot of corruption, dishonesty and other things going on and there always will be. However our government is very big business and just like anything else, big businesses have a tendency to have a lot of things 'fall through the cracks' as they say.

Unfortunately it's a one sided game though, and the players need to forfeit. The players I speak of are the smoking public and it's a roll of the dice. It's like playing roulette with a 6-shooter…only the odds are much worse. There is only one thing that we know for sure: You can only win by not playing.

Here's something else I read on the Internet concerning smoking, and I quote: *"Do you do bad things? Even though you know you shouldn't? It's not your fault. It really isn't. You know you should stop doing it, but no matter how much you know that, and how much you try, you just can't stop!"*

Crap I say! This is absolutely amazing! That is exactly what advertising agencies want to hear. Again, they get paid millions of dollars annually by the tobacco companies. Why? To make you believe that it's not your fault and you can't help it. The American smoking public needs to wise up and pay attention to what's being programmed into that gray matter between the ears. I'll talk about this a little later but basically, if you consciously look at advertisements and commercials, the presuppositions are absolutely ludicrous. Do not fall into the trap of pointing the finger and tell yourself that you can't help but smoke. You smoke because you choose to. A very wise man once said this: "Every time you point a finger, three fingers and a thumb come back at the problem." I've never forgotten that and it had to be 8 years ago that I first heard it. He also asked, "Have ever looked in the mirror and said, hello stupid." All I'm saying here is just be big enough to take responsibility for your actions, and if they're less than perfect then hey, welcome to the human race.

2

A Dying Breed

The Lost Cause

I read an article that said, in so many words, that smokers are of less then average intelligence. I was livid after reading it; that is until I digested it and realized that it very well could be the truth. If you don't think that smokers are a dying breed, here are a few selections to show just a small portion of the U.S. Government Regulations that have been implemented over the years. If you need to, re-read these a couple times if you don't understand them because education and understanding is a big part of the arsenal of anyone ready to become an ex-smoker.

1967—Federal Communications Commission rules that the Fairness Doctrine applies to cigarette advertising. Stations broadcasting cigarette commercials must donate airtime to antismoking messages.

1971—Fairness Doctrine antismoking messages end when cigarette advertising is prohibited on radio and television.

1973—Civil Aeronautics Board requires no-smoking sections on all commercial airline flights.

1987—Department of Health and Human Services establishes a smoke free environment in its facilities.

1992—Federal Trade Commission takes first enforcement action under the Comprehensive Smokeless Tobacco Health Education Act, alleging that Pinkerton Tobacco Company's Red Man brand name appeared illegally during a televised event.

1993—Environmental Protection Agency releases final risk assessment on environmental tobacco smoke (ETS) and classifies ETS as a "Group A" (known human) carcinogen.

1994—Occupational Safety and Health Administration announces proposed regulation to prohibit smoking in the workplace, except in separately ventilated smoking rooms.

1994—Department of Defense (DOD) bans smoking in DOD workplaces.

1995—Department of Justice reaches a settlement with Philip Morris to remove tobacco advertisements from the line of sight of television cameras in sports stadiums. Also, President Clinton announces the publication of the Food and Drug Administration's proposed regulations that would restrict the sale, distribution, and marketing of cigarettes and smokeless tobacco products to protect children and adolescents.

1996—President Clinton announces the nation's first comprehensive program to prevent children and adolescents from smoking cigarettes or using smokeless tobacco and beginning a lifetime of nicotine addiction. With the August 1996 publication of a final rule on tobacco in the Federal Register, the Food and Drug Administration (FDA) will regulate the sale and distribution of cigarettes and smokeless tobacco to children and adolescents. The provisions of the FDA rule are aimed at reducing youth access to tobacco products and the appeal of tobacco advertising to young people. Additionally, the FDA will propose to require the major tobacco companies to educate young people about the real health dangers associated with tobacco use through a multimedia campaign.

1997—President Clinton announces an Executive Order to make all federal workplaces smoke-free.

Seeing the forest through the trees

And here's some from the U.S. Legislation:

In 1965 the *Federal Cigarette Labeling and Advertising Act* required package warning label—"Caution: Cigarette Smoking May Be Hazardous to Your Health." It required no labels on cigarette advertisements. It also required the FTC to report to Congress annually on the effectiveness of cigarette labeling, current cigarette advertising and promotion practices. It required Department of Health, Education, and Welfare (DHEW) to report annually to Congress on the health consequences of smoking.

Then in 1969 the *Public Health Cigarette Smoking Act* required package warning label that says, "Warning: The Surgeon General Has Determined that Cigarette Smoking Is Dangerous to Your Health." So here they went from 'may be' to 'is'. They also prohibited cigarette advertising on television and radio. The Department of Justice then prevents States or localities from regulating or prohibiting cigarette advertising or promotion for health-related reasons.

Then the Controlled Substances Act of 1970 prevents the abuse of drugs, narcotics, and other addictive substances and specifically excludes tobacco from the definition of a "controlled substance." I'm sure that was funded by the tobacco companies.

Then in 1972, Consumer Product Safety Act transferred authority from the FDA to regulate hazardous substances as designated by the Federal Hazardous Substances Labeling Act (FHSA) to the Consumer Product Safety Commission.

The Little Cigar Act of 1973 banned little cigar advertisements from television and radio. The 1976 amendment to the Federal Hazardous Substances Labeling Act of 1960 says that the term "hazardous substance" shall not apply to tobacco and tobacco products (passed when the American Public Health Association petitioned CPSC to set a maximum level of 21 mg. of tar in cigarettes).

The object of the Toxic Substances Control Act of 1976 was to "regulate chemical substances and mixtures which present an unreasonable risk of injury to health or the environment" and of course the term "chemical substance" does not include tobacco or any tobacco products.

Then in 1984 the Comprehensive Smoking Education Act institutes four rotating health warning labels (all listed as Surgeon General's Warnings) on cigarette packages and advertisements (smoking causes lung cancer, heart disease and may complicate pregnancy; quitting smoking now greatly reduces serious risks to your health; smoking by pregnant women may result in fetal injury, premature birth, and low birth weight; cigarette smoke contains carbon monoxide). It also requires the Department of Health and Human Services (DHHS) to publish a biennial status report to Congress on smoking and health. Additionally, it requires cigarette industry to provide a confidential list of ingredients added to cigarettes manufactured in or imported into the United States (brand-specific ingredients and quantities not required). So the chemical injection begins.

The Cigarette Safety Act of 1984 is to determine technical and commercial feasibility of developing cigarettes and little cigars that would be less likely to ignite upholstered furniture and mattresses.

The Comprehensive Smokeless Tobacco Health Education Act of 1986 institutes three rotating health-warning labels on smokeless tobacco packages and advertisements (this product may cause mouth cancer; this product may cause gum disease and tooth loss; this product is not a safe alternative to cigarettes) except billboards.

And on and on…the list is nearly endless.

3

The Product

Do you really know what's in those things?

I began most days while I was quitting by getting some good information online and reading the postings from my quit smoking support group. Then I read this article about how the federal government approves for the tobacco companies to put any combination of over 599 additives at random into cigarette tobacco, all of which are approved, yes by our United States Government. Why 599, why not 600? I don't get it either, but here's a few that that I just jotted down:

Ammoniated Glycyrrhizin
Decanis Acid
Dehydromenthofurolactone
Dihydro Anethole
Ethoxybenzaldehyde
Ethyl Acetate
Ethyl Alcohol
Ethyl Benzoate
Ethyl Decanoate
Ethyl Propionate
Farnesol
Furfuryl
Glutamic Acid
Heptanoic Acid
Heptyl Acetate
Hexyl Acetate

Isoamyl Butyrate
Isoamyl Phenylacetate
Isobornyl Acetate
Isobutyl Alcohol
Isobutyl Salicylate
Isobutyraldehyde
Isobutyric Acid
Isovaleric Acid
Lactic Acid
Levulinic Acid
Linalyl Acetate
Magnesium Carbonate
Malic Acid
Methyl Benzoate
Methyl Sulfide
Methyl Thiophenecarboxaldehyde
Methyl Heptadien
Methyl Vinylthiazole

…And that's only 25 of them, there are 574 others! Look them up in the internet yourself; don't take my word for it. Just use the keywords "599 additives" in any internet browser and read away!

Here's an interesting fact, and the scariest thought of this whole thing: While these ingredients are approved as additives for foods, they were not tested by burning them. However, it's the burning of many of these substances, which obviously changes their properties, and then turns them into deadly gases and such. And yes, our government approved these…all of them. But how is that possible because in the preceding chapter, it seems that they're looking out for us doesn't it? Well, if the right hand doesn't know what the left hand is doing, we're bound to have a mess. Talk about falling between the cracks! There are over 4000 chemical compounds created by burning a cigarette, many of which are toxic and/or carcinogenic. If you don't know what that means, talk to someone that went to military boot camp. We got the honor and privilege of inhaling these types of gases as part of our training in the infamous 'Gas Chamber' and trust me, it's something that you don't forget. Carbon monoxide, nitrogen oxides, hydrogen cyanide and ammonia are all present in cigarette smoke. Forty-three known carcinogens are in that pretty blue smoke that peacefully drifts up to the heavens. It's chilling to think about not only how smokers poison themselves, but also what others are exposed to that are breathing in the secondhand smoke. The next time you light one up, take a good long look at this list and see them for what they are: *a delivery system for toxic chemicals and carcinogens that will eventually kill you in a very slow and painful way.*

Where's the trust?

No wonder people are becoming more interested in researching the tobacco companies. They're nothing but dishonest, greedy, powerful, deceitful and just downright evil and people need to know the truth. There something wrong here when you read that urine contains something called urea, which is sometimes added to cigarette tobacco (isn't that just yummy). Another is that the impact of nicotine is jacked up because tobacco companies add ammonia. Plain old tobacco with all its wonders and all the damage it causes isn't enough, so they add ammonia, of course with the approval of our government. Here's another one: Cigarette smoke contains benzene, carbon monoxide, arsenic and hydrogen cyanide. It also contains Polonium 210, which had been found to be a radioactive isotope. I could write for a year with the amount of information that's out there.

They love our kids too

Here are some interesting facts concerning our children: Every day about 2000 youths become daily smokers. Every year cigarettes leave about 31,000 kids without Dads; yes they die. Every year approximately 4,400 kids between the ages of 12 and 17 try a cigarette for the first time. Tobacco companies make $2.2 billion a year from under age sales (from 2003 stats). And until I became consciously aware of it I never realized that tobacco signage is often placed at a child's eye level.

And it just gets better…

- Cigarette smoking causes significant health problems among children and adolescents, including coughing, shortness of breath, production of phlegm, respiratory illnesses, reduced physical fitness, poorer lung growth and function, and worse health overall.
- The younger they begin to smoke the more likely they are to be an adult smoker. Not only that, young people who start smoking at an earlier age are more likely to develop long-term nicotine addiction than people who start later in life.
- Only 3% of high school smokers think they will be smoking in 5 years, but in reality, studies show that 40% to 50% will still be smoking 7 or 8 years later.
- Each day, more than 4,000 teens try their first cigarette, and another 2,000 become regular, daily smokers. Of those, 1 out of 3 will eventually die from smoking-related disease.
- Most teen smokers report that they would like to quit and have made unsuccessful attempts to do so. Those who try to quit smoking report withdrawal symptoms similar to those reported by adults.
- Adolescent tobacco users are more likely to use alcohol and illegal drugs than are nonusers.
- Cigarette smokers are also more likely to get into fights, carry weapons, attempt suicide, suffer from mental health problems such as depression, and engage in high-risk sexual behaviors.
- Each year, the tobacco industry must replace its many consumers who either quit smoking or who die from smoking-related diseases. Where do most of these new consumers come from? From the ranks of our children.
- Nationwide, about 28% of high school students reported using some type of tobacco (cigarette, cigar, pipe or smokeless tobacco).
- On average, more than 22% of students smoked cigarettes in 2003.

- About 7% of high school students reported using smokeless tobacco at least once. Male students were 27% more likely to use smokeless tobacco than female students.

Is this what our children are destined for? What are we doing to help with this? I have a 9 year old at home and although I cannot shelter him form life, he is 39% to 46% less likely to smoke because I've quit. We need to do what we can even if it's only setting an example. Join me…break the chains.

Legal homicide

Death is a big business. The coroner is paid well, the mortician, the caskets sell for a fortune but this one is staggering. The one thing that still sets me off into an emotional frenzy is even after all the studies, all the knowledge that this stuff is killing us, all the organizations out there that are willing to help us, this fact that is still mind boggling to me is this: Tobacco kills more Americans than AIDS, drugs, homicides, fires and auto accidents combined. And you know where it all starts? With the young people, that's where. Get them stated young right? They're called replacement smokers…isn't that nice?

Do you see why I have an attitude? Maybe you should get one too.

4

Scrupulous Advertising

Billion dollar programming

Have you ever seen a beer commercial? That's stupid, of course you have. Advertising in the United States runs around the hundred billion dollar range. And don't ever doubt that they make that money back. They show mountains and talk about the crystal clear waters of the Colorado Rockies. Delivering the message in an eloquent manner is a middle-aged gentleman who's good looking with perfect teeth. He's dressed in a flannel shirt that has just been pressed, there's not a silver hair out of place on his head, and the coat is suede with a big furry collar. He tells you about the barley, hops and how it's cold-brewed to perfection. In the background you see the mountain range that's worthy of any Thomas Kincade print, his beautiful home on a range with a picket fence. Out back in the field there's the most beautiful thoroughbred that money can buy. He tells you about his family business that's been around for generations. Then how much they take pride in their product and that they would never let you down with poor quality so it's safe to buy their beer. Here's what they're telling the audience: All I have to do is drink this stuff and I'm going have a house like that in the mountains, I'll have that horse, I'll have that view in my back yard and when I'm middle-aged I'll look just like that guy. It's a fairy tale and this sounds so ridiculous it's rather pathetic. So tell me then, why does it work? I can tell you that it works because people are looking for that same sensation when they drink the product, as what they saw in that fairy tale in the commercial. They're trying to program us and it's irrelevant whether you believe it or not…because it's true. And if you go research the numbers you'll see that advertising just flat out works. Don't take my word for it.

Shut up brain; look at what we'll get

How about a Michelob commercial? They show you young ladies with zero body fat, perfect legs, complexions that are stunning and boyfriends that look the same. The people in the background are all near perfect physical specimens. The good looking, dark-haired guy on the pool table is being hit on by the most gorgeous creature to walk the planet. Even the bartender is good looking, with that perfect smile, as he tosses the bottle in the air only to catch it behind his back as everyone cheers him on. So here they are drinking a Michelob with some rockin blues music playing in the background. Everybody is laughing, having a great time and the bar is spotless. No body is spilling drinks on anybody's girlfriend. Okay let's stop right there and talk reality here. The truth of the matter is if you're a guy and you go have a Michelob at a local bar, you will be hit on but not like you think, and she won't be little Miss Gorgeous either. It'll be some bar fly that's half tanked with stinky beer breath, probably cigarette breath too and nearly falling down. Or if you're a gal, get excited about beer belly Barney with beer burps and a booger hanging out of one of his nostrils because he forgot to clip those darn nose hairs again. Okay, I'm being a little sarcastic but here's a fair question then: Why don't they show you the puke in the bathroom all over the floor and your roommate sleeping in it because he got hammered last night? Or the girl that got pregnant because she was so toasted that some jerk took advantage of her. Hey, all I'm saying is let's look at the real picture here because that commercial isn't it, nor are any of them.

Look, I'm not bagging on the beer companies. Personally I prefer Gin but my point is this: There's very little difference between the advertising of the beer companies, and the advertising the tobacco companies do, it's just a different product, and the tobacco companies are restricted to a point, and thank God. Remember Joe Camel? Let me tell you what he did for the massive R.J. Reynolds tobacco company. That little sax-playing dude is credited with boosting sales for R.J. Reynolds's Camel brand that eventually became the seventh-best-selling cigarette in the United States. Originally he started killing people in France, but then R.J. Reynolds imported Joe Camel to the United States in the late 80's. Joe Camel eventually became the catalyst for criticism that was endorsed by President Clinton's anti-underage-smoking initiatives. Here's a gem for you: There were reports that proved that found children were as likely to recognize Joe Camel as they were Mickey Mouse (but they don't advertise to youths, right?). Additionally, another report found a significant increase in adolescent smoking after the launch of the Camel character. R.J. Reynolds denies allegations that it was catering to children, but the reports speak volumes to make them look like the lying dirt bags that they are.

Advertising, lying…what's the difference?

I never saw the Joe Camel on a poster where he's in a hospital room with an iron lung because he can't breathe, withering away due to cancer. They only show him with a saxophone playing his heart out in from of a group of people that make him out to be a god. Okay I understand that he was a cartoon character but the Marlboro Man was not. Did you ever see him sitting on his deathbed, weighing 95 pounds with tubes in ever orifice waiting to die from cancer and other tobacco related illnesses due to smoking cigarettes? Of course not…why should they show the other half of the story? I'm old enough to remember the commercials on television that made smoking look grown up, sophisticated and mature. I smoked Newport and if you look at the ads still in some magazines, they still portray it as sexy and appealing with those good looking guys, those foxy girls going for a ride on that beautiful 25-foot sailboat…amazing! Also, they still advertise through media like movies although it's far less common. Here's a good one for you to chew on: Philip Morris, the tobacco monster I spoke of earlier, paid $350,000 so that their brand of cigarettes would be shown in the James Bond movie "Licensed to Kill." Mind you this was just to show them! Philip Morris also paid $42,500 to have its Marlboro cigarette appear in the movie "Superman II." Understand again, that's just to show it on screen for a blip of time! Another cigarette manufacturer, Liggett, paid $30,000 to have its cigarettes appear in the movie "Supergirl." Now note that although this was a while back, these are movies that are targeting child and adolescent audiences. But the tobacco companies assure us that they're playing by the rules. I can't write what I truly think, but you get the idea.

Here's a few more just for good measure:

- Cigarette advertising boosts consumption. One report from the FDA, which was prepared with the cooperation of the tobacco industry, concludes "advertising was found to have a statistically significant impact on industry sales."
- Among children aged 10 and 11 years over 80% of them believe that cigarette advertising encourages children to start smoking.
- Cigarette advertisements portray smoking as a normal, healthy, fun-filled activity. This undermines the message from parents and teachers that smoking causes death and disease leaving out youth befuddled.
- A major scientific analysis of all the literature on the effects of cigarette advertising concluded that "a preponderance of quantitative studies of cigarette advertising suggest a causal relationship with consumption."
- It has been proven that children smoke the most heavily advertised brands of cigarettes (but again, they don't advertise to out kids…yeah, okay!).
- In Australia, the advertising efforts on the part of the Peter Jackson cigarette brand are reflected in its rise from 1% of the adolescent market in 1993 to 37% in 1997.
- Tobacco sponsorship of sport acts as cigarette advertising to children. The children who watch the sporting events on television readily recognize those cigarette brands that sponsored the event.
- Among children aged 10 and 11 years, more than 65% of them believed that tobacco sponsorship of sport is another form of cigarette advertising.

- Nearly nine out of ten (87%) of children aged between 10 and 15 think that the models in cigarette advertisements are under 25 years old.

Underage smoking is, for the most part, due to the fact that they spend more on advertising than most of us can even comprehend. It's deceitful, cheating, lying and just evil. All we can do to is try to set an example for our youngsters. It's all the little things that we need to be aware of for ourselves as well. So what does this have to do with you? Well, it worked on you so if we begin to understand it from an intellectual point of view, we'll have a better chance to reverse the programming and break the chains.

PART II
The Memories

5

Learn to move on

Skeletons

I read that the average person quits 4.2 times before they succeed. Then I read 3.2 times but either way, very few do it on the first try although it can be done. Who cares how many times you fail as long as you succeed? Here's one for you: How long would you let your son or daughter try riding a bike until you said, "forget it, you'll never get it." You'd never say that, at least I hope not! You'd tell them to get back on and try again. This is exactly the same thing. It's no different here. If you're reading this book, that most likely means that you've quit in the past and for whatever reason you relapsed and here you are. Here's the important thing to do: Just remember whatever you did that aided you in your initial success and use that this time. Okay take a bowler that tries to get a strike every single time they throw the ball. But listen to this; from my calculations it took me just over 20,000 games to bowl my first perfect 300 game. Was I a failure? Before you answer it's only fair to tell you that I had a 217 average that year, 1984 if you're curious, and made my share of tournament prize monies. Now you can answer, was I a failure? I don't think so. You probably already know that Thomas Edison tried 20,000 times to create the light bulb before succeeding. Now back to you. So, the last time you quit, did you tell everybody that you were quitting? If you did then don't this time! If you never stop trying you'll succeed eventually. You already know these things so don't even go there. All you did last time you failed is discovered the things, or combination of things that didn't work. Move on.

Judge not…

You probably have already drummed up those thoughts from the past when you tried and missed the boat. There is a variable involved in all quitters and that variable is the amount of conviction they have. I remember my past attempts were all only half efforts compared to the time that I succeeded. Victory will not be denied for those that are ready for the challenge and can manage their way through the judgment variables. Remember that conviction is a variable. It's important that you understand why I call it that. There are two reasons: (1) It changes from person to person depending on where they are in their life and how ready they are and (2) It changes for a period of time after you quit due the addictive properties/chemicals of the cigarettes. The first week or so you will rationalize everything which is where you're conviction is tested. You will feel as strong as a giant one minute, then the next you feel like giving up. Realize that every time you stay strong and say no just one more time, you will be gaining ground on your goal. Remember: *The resolve gets stronger with time for those that succeed.* You will succeed if you don't prejudge yourself from past performances. Those were just practice runs. Anyone can relate to that even if we're talking about throwing darts, playing golf or whatever.

Seeing Red

One of my past quits that ultimately failed but stood for around 18 months was a good learning tool. I was smoking Kools. Yes, that nasty menthol brand that makes even the most loyal smokers say "Yuk!" Here's what happened: Early in the morning I'm in my bathroom having a bad coughing episode so I was leaning over the toilet thinking I might gag. Then to my surprise up comes this thing that looked like a piece to skin. It was very thin and about one inch in diameter. The kicker is that it was covered in blood. Fear is amazing emotion because I threw the cigarettes in the trash and didn't smoke for over 18 months. What made me start up again? Peer pressure. I was only 19 years old. I think of all the money I could've saved and all the hell I would have avoided had I just stayed clean. Another time I quit for about 4 months. I remember that I cut gradually that time and because it wasn't permanent, I knew that this wouldn't be my method of choice. That was in 1986. All the subsequent attempts were all only half efforts as I call them. You know, the New Year's Eve kind that don't mean squat usually.

So make a mental note of what you did last time that hindered your efforts, and write down what helped you. Understand what you're going to do this time and what you're going to change. Make a list of benefits on a tiny little post it note and carried it in your wallet, or take a walk every day at a certain time; or avoid certain people if you need to. Trust me, they'll get over it. That may sound harsh but hey, we're talking about your life here. I did the list in the wallet 6 weeks prior to quitting and every time I opened my wallet to either get out a credit card, or cash, I would take it out and read it quickly. That may seem insignificant but remember; we're looking for the combination of all these things to work together. That's the key…finding a winning combination.

The Bare Bones

Don't beat yourself up over the past…and I've done it too. I mean I've quit before then beat myself up mentally for months because I started up again. Don't waste the energy…save it and use it for something constructive. And there were certain times in my life that had me convinced I would never be able to quit. But a lot can be said about persistence and tenacity. Most relapses occur within 3 months and half the battle is being aware of that fact. It doesn't matter what happened yesterday, last month or last year. It only matters that you move forward. Screw the past!

Most people that I've talked to either in person, or on the Internet have told me that they too, for months, and some like me, some for years, have thought daily about quitting. What keeps them from taking on the task is simply fear of failure. Funny though of you think that the worst thing that can happen is that you fail, then try again using the successful things that you've used in the past, canning the bad ideas and moving forward. That's it. Well, if that's it then what's the big deal? I'll tell you what. We think that we relinquish control and every time we fail, we don't look at it as a stepping-stone, which is precisely what it really is. We look at ourselves as weak and not in control. Change that false perception and we grow stronger every time if we feed the mind or fail to quit. It's just a matter of looking at it the right way.

6

Beware of experts

Be careful who you listen to

Let's be realistic here. If you want to learn how to be a great swimmer you don't go to a wrestling coach. If you want to know how to have a good marriage, you don't go to someone that's been divorced 4 times and on their 5th marriage. Tell me why then would someone ask advice on how to quit smoking from people that smoke? Or even from people that have never smoked? I've seen it on both sides and it never seizes to amaze me every single time I see it. If you want to quit smoking, or take on anything talk to people that have been there. Talk to ex-smokers that have succeeded and have stayed clean. If you talk to these people, you will be blown away at their enthusiasm to help and encourage you. Don't talk to the person that says, "Yup I gave them up 12 years ago and I still want one." That person needs a slap in the head because not only will they eventually smoke again; they are trying to make you feel as if it's too difficult. Either way—turn and run from these idiots and leave them to wallow in their own miserable existence.

Here's another breed that you need to be aware of and I'll start with a question: If someone has a PHD and has studied smoking behaviors, although they never touched a cigarette in their life, why does that make them an expert on quitting smoking? I'll answer for you: *It doesn't!* I see books that are written by Stanford graduates of whatever and what they think is that because they went to an expensive school, learned the system and how to pass (notice I didn't say anything about learning there), all of a sudden they are an expert on what it takes to quit smoking and possibly

Nuclear Physics too! That would be like me writing a book on how to restore a car. I've never done it but hey, who cares right? Seriously, I was a 27-year smoker and I believe with all my heart, I can help anyone that wants to quit smoking achieve that goal. Why? It's because I went through it. Just a little common sense here is all you need. If you talk to those that tried and failed, all you'll get is what does not work. If you talk to those that have never smoked, they'll probably be supportive but in a nice, clueless way. You don't need someone full of their own ignorance any more that you need negative input so just search for the truth. It's out there….everywhere.

Talk with people at your work that used to smoke. Ask around and don't be afraid and you will find undying support from near strangers. You'll also be amazed at how many folks out there used to smoke! I met a person that was smoke free for 12 years and she was amazingly excited for me and my upcoming journey. It's amazing how many people that people like her just encourage people like us. Talk with them on how they did it, what method they used, did they use a smoking cessation program, how they made it through the first week and whatever else you can think of. One lady did tell me that she used a smoking cessation program. Then amazingly enough, she also told me that I could just save the money and I'd be fine. Apparently she wasn't impressed with it at all. She probably saved me a couple hundred dollars. Anyway, you get the picture. When you've succeed and you are smoke free for a decent period of time, and you meet someone that's in the process of quitting, or planning to quit, there is an instant bond. It's like you're kindred spirits or something that's hard to explain. Just like they are doing for you, so will you do for others when you're smoke-free. You're going to be so excited for them, you're going to encourage them and that to me, is one of the most awesome things to be able to do for someone that's struggling with something so difficult to cease. It's the human spirit, which is exactly what prompted me to write this book.

Go to your doctor if you need an extra push. Mine was great. All he did, which is all he had to do is say in a soft, calm and straight forward voice,

"It will catch up with you eventually." He said that to me every time I visited. He never mentioned smoking because he knew that I knew exactly what he meant. I love him for that.

Where's the love?

Another group is family and friends, but be careful with this because of the emotional attachment. I would like to believe that everyone's family would support them but unfortunately that's not always the case. If that's your situation then stick with your friends. I also know that there may be people, some family or close friends that would rather see you fail because that way, they feel that their own smoking habit is justified. Steer clear of them until you've proven yourself and who knows, you may be the spark that they need to push them into giving them up too. What a deal that would be.

Some people prefer to tell everyone. As a matter of fact, all the PHDs that I mentioned earlier say that this is a must. Well, I hate to disagree but all I can say is balderdash! I told nobody! Why? Because every other time I tried I did just what they said, told everyone, then failed. I felt extreme pressure using that method so I figured that I had nothing to loose by doing just the opposite by telling not telling a soul. Interestingly enough, I confide in my wife for everything and I didn't even tell her until my third day. I just wanted to succeed…and I know you do too. If you told people before, then don't this time. Try the method of telling no one until you've been clean for a few days. Then when you do finally tell them, watch their faces light up with excitement for your victory.

7

The sweet nectar of victory

Irrelevant time

Regardless of what you may have heard, read or learned from the so called experts, the length of time you've smoke it irrelevant. I'm sorry but if you smoke a pack a day and have been smoking for 20 years, you are no different that the person who smokes a pack a day for 10 years, or 40 years. It just doesn't matter. However, the amount you smoke per day surely is relevant, but again and more important is the conviction level of the person involved. I have a ridiculously simple method that I will show you that can help anybody cut your smoking down from 25% to 40% right now…immediately! I know the goal is to quit, but this is just part of the process (remember I said it's a process), a means to an end, with the goal of quitting in mind. Here are a few stories, all of which are 100% true, which should speak volumes.

The straw that broke the camels back

My father smoked for 27 years, which is rather peculiar that he and I both quit after the same number of years. This is a rather funny story that's definitely worth sharing. This was one of those rare instances where someone just quits…out of the blue. There was no planning…any thought…nothing. So here's the scene: He and I were in the car going to a bowling tournament. I don't remember where we bowled because we didn't do very well that weekend. Anyway, we were traveling along one of the New York State's Thruways. There were two packs of Lark cigarettes on the seat, one opened and one un-opened. He didn't see the one that was opened so he opened the un-opened pack, lit up and was happy. I wondered why and mentioned to him that there was already an opened pack on the seat and I didn't understand why he opened a new one. The answer was obvious when he looked at me because it was then that I realized that he didn't see the pack that was already opened. And for some reason that set him off. He got extremely upset with himself, and as the old adage says, "That was the straw that broke the camel's back." He threw the lit cigarette out the window, threw the 2 packs of Larks over his shoulder into the back seat looked at me and said, "That's it. I'm not smoking anymore." I thought that he was just irritated at himself but with God as my witness, he never smoked another cigarette in his life…ever! That's the power of a decision. Look up the origin of the word 'decide' and you'll find that it means 'to cut off from.' There's power in a decision when it's made from within…just like my Dad did that day on the Thruway.

Old Smokey

My Father-in-Law smoked like a chimney for over 40 years. It caused him to be diagnosed with emphysema. His doctor told him to quit, or die very soon and by using a smoke cessation program he was able to successfully quit. As of this writing is alive and well, and smoke free and lives a nice retired lifestyle in the mid-West. He is a very compulsive person and that's not to slam him at all. That's just to say you could set your watch to him having his next cigarette and he must have smoked at least 2 packs a day. He would smoke in his car in the middle of the winter with the windows rolled up (Yuk!) and just puff away! His car smelled disgustingly like an ashtray filled with water, I mean literally! I absolutely knew that if he could do it, I could also do it.

A Class Act

This is a rather personal story but one that must be told. My wife was a smoker for 12 years before she quit. Now I know I'm a little bias here but she is an amazing woman and I am blessed to have her as a partner in this crazy world. Years ago, we were trying to have a child and there were issues that took me having to have surgery to resolve. I had the surgery, all was well and we just wanted to have our little one. Anyhow, she was smoking about a pack a day or so when she found out that she was pregnant with our miracle baby was in her womb. And you know what that classy lady did? Threw those lousy things in the trash and hasn't smoked since. Now that's the power of a decision.

Little by little

As for me, I was a 27-year smoker. I smoked somewhere around a pack a day, give or take a few. I didn't have one of those life-changing moments like my Dad. My commitment came gradually over the course of time, but I thank God that it finally came. My son was 8 years old when I quit and he never saw me with a cigarette in my mouth…ever. I hid it from him because I was ashamed and didn't want him to see me smoking. I knew that if he saw me, he'd say to himself, "Well I guess it's not that bad; Dad does it." I had quit about 5 or 6 times over the years, some half-heartedly, before finally succeeding, but I did finally succeed, just like you will. The older I got the more I thought about it and realized that it was just a matter of time until it gets the best of me. And every time I lit up, for about the last 2 years of smoking, I thought about it. And I mean every single time. That's a whole lot of thinking which began to change my perspective over time. I've been free for a long time now and if I could only put the conviction inside me into others, the tobacco companies would be flat busted. I've learned one thing that I tell everyone that's trying to quit and that's this:

The resolve gets stronger with time for those that succeed.

You probably don't fully understand the significance of this statement. I will promise you one thing: If you put this up on your bathroom mirror, and read it after you have been free from tobacco for even just a month, you will have a whole new perspective on its relevance.

The good fight

So, what's your story? How long have you been smoking cigarettes? Do the math. Figure out how many you've smoked since you started and then figure out the cost in dollars but not for a year, since you started. Now go throw up thinking about all that money. Then you just have to decide. Is it really that simple? Yes but like I said, it's a personal thing. With me it had to build over time. With my Dad and wife, they just said "I'm done." If you're like me you probably have people breathing down your neck and although this doesn't help a bit, they think it does. Just love them anyhow for the thought. It doesn't matter how long you've smoked because once the habit is there, even if you've only smoked for a short time, breaking it is like trying to un-break a glass that's dropped on the floor. It can be done, but it is just a little difficult. All I'm saying here it this: It doesn't matter that you're a 5 year smoker, 40 year smoker, a heavy smoker, a light smoker, a compulsive smoker or an occasional smoker…nothing matters other than your willingness to pick up this book, or any other book for that matter, so you can educate yourself and gather the weapons to win this fight. *And make no mistake; this is a fight.* If you don't think this is a fight for your life, you might want to rethink why you're reading this.

8

What's your take?

Do you believe?

No, I'm not talking about God....*yet*. I'm going to ask you a question and I want you to be totally honest. Do you sincerely believe that you can quit? This isn't about me or anybody else, it's about you. You need to be honest with yourself with this one and you know what? If you decide that the answer at this point in time is *no*, that's okay because it will change eventually. You know how I know that? Because you're reading this and if I could give you a hug I would (sorry, it's the Italian in me and I wouldn't change it for anything). Do you really want to quit? Is it in your heart? Is it in your soul? Do you feel it? If you answered yes that I promise you my friend, you will. But you have to be ready. As I mentioned earlier, I had so many people hounding me to quit and I just wanted them to leave me the hell alone! You know why? Because I wasn't ready yet and here's a tip, I knew that, they did not. So I just kept doing my research, something I'll talk about later in the book, and when I was ready, I succeeded and so will you. You may be ready now, but if not, don't panic, just keep the faith. And I'm telling you that a commitment filled with faith and belief will eventually manifest itself inside you.

You have heard this before but here goes: *Whether you believe you can or believe you cannot, you're absolutely right.* This is truly an amazing statement that is so simple it's rather sickening. But you know what? This is the purest form of reassurance you have to know that this is not wasted effort. If you believe you can conquer this thing, you will.

You can to anything that you want to do in this life. I felt so helpless for years and felt as if I could never live without these stupid tobacco sticks. Then, little by little, things changed. Let me tell you something that you already know: It doesn't matter what anybody else says if you believe. I swear to you this one is true: I had a guy sitting in the cube behind me, temporarily, at my work place. I was in my first week of quitting. I was a little on edge and everyone else was very supportive, other than this particular person. So this is what this bozo says to me on my fourth day of being smoke free; "You aren't going to make it. I can't believe that you're trying to quit. Why are you bothering?" I saw red and my Italian temper came through for me. I cannot repeat in this book what I said to him but I will tell you that not only did this motivate me towards victory; he didn't speak to me for about a week because I verbally put him in his place. Now, I'm not a tough guy but that was just a cold thing to do that to another human being that's struggling to better their life. And I hope that you will rip someone's head off too if they dare put you down for having the guts to do this. And interestingly, he wasn't a smoker.

Bowled over

At one point in my life, I was a very good bowler. Actually I was once a professional caliber bowler, holding about a 220 average. Now, I only tell you that to tell you this: It took me a long time to believe in my heart that I could hold that kind of average. It took physical practice, belief, thought filtering and watching what my self-talk was. I also believed that I would someday throw a perfect game, which I finally did in 1984. Why? Because I believed, in fact I just knew that I would.

Belief is nothing more than faith in the unseen. If you didn't fervently believe that you can kick this habit, I doubt you would be reading this book.

Go onto the Internet and read about all the people that have kicked this habit successfully. There are thousands of testimonials and I promise that you will find some that will not only blow your mind; they will inspire you because you'll also see that anyone can do this. Some of them even lost lungs before they finally quit. Yes, regardless of what you've read about this habit, anyone can do this if given the right tools, information, motivation and they actually want it…in their heart.

But how?

The seeds of thought that you put into your mind will dictate whether you succeed or fail. And those seeds of thought are controlled by what you believe. You may have to train your mind to believe. Let's first define belief: (1) To accept as true or real; (2) To credit with veracity (truth); (3) To expect or suppose; (4) To have faith, confidence, or trust; (5) To have confidence in the truth of something.

You must filter your thoughts. You may have to dump some smoker friends for a while. You must practice healthy self-talk. Everybody does self-talk, even if you don't really speak out loud. It's that little voice saying, "You can't do it." When that happens, you must override that evil by *saying aloud*, "Oh yeah, you watch me!" You must fervently believe. Do you know how many times I heard that little pesky negative voice the night I bowled my 300 game? Not once. You want to know why? Because I trained my mind, at least in that area of my life, to completely shut out anything other than the "I can" thoughts; and even then it was still very difficult at times. Because it takes conscious effort to do and most of us have been taught what we cannot do; not what we can do. Additionally, and unfortunately, most people are basically negative due to the nature of our society.

You must fervently believe because nothing good can be accomplished without that conviction. There is a power in self-talk; understand it and use it. Filter your thoughts and make sure they benefit you. Also, you can speak what you want into existence if you truly believe. And through conscious effort, you can instill the will to quit into yourself, and all that's required is conscious effort linked to purpose.

PART III
The Support

9

Only the strong survive

Strength in Unity

Okay, a support network is something that we all need in many different areas of our lives. Those that decide not to get involved are only hurting themselves. Hear me out: If you were in college, sometimes study groups would be your support group if you needed help with a certain area, or just wanted to do well. Or if you're a competitive racquetball player then you're study group would be who you practice with. If you were a computer geek, your support group would be the chat room where all the other geeks could swap ideas, fixes and what not. If you're a young church going person, your youth group may be your support group to keep you on the path you'd like to pursue. All these groups help keep us on track with a specific goal in mind. They're not just for people with vices such as smoking or drinking. They're for anyone and everyone, in any walk of life that either wants to excel at something or just stay on the right track. There is strength in unity, don't ever doubt it.

Your Log Book

You're not going to log anything just yet, that comes later but I want you to be aware of the concept when I bring it up in Part 6. When I was bowling way back in the 70's, I actually kept a log of what spares I missed the most so when I practiced the following week, I would focus more attention on those spares. In addition, during tournaments, I kept a log of different lane reactions corresponding with the lane number so when it came for the 'head to head' competition, even if it was the next day, I would still have a good idea of my ball reaction before even starting thereby giving myself the best chance of winning. That's all you're going to do with your smoking: By recognizing patterns, you give yourself the best chance to succeed because they then become evident. Then once you're aware of the patterns, you'll be amazed at how easy it is to make small changes without too much trouble at all.

Your Journal

There is power in the written word. Just look at the Bible. If you're going to take this seriously then getting a journal is a must. This is one of those things that the PHDs say to do that I actually agree with. And this little book can be your best friend in the whole world. Rather than write down where and when you smoke, write down your emotional reasoning as to why you're going to go have that cigarette, and then go have it. The goal here is rather than do something out of pure habit without even considering what you're doing; you just need to look at the actions. Try for a moment looking at it from the outside, where you're looking into your life through a window. Notice what you do, how you do it, and why (if there's even a reason). Are you even thinking? Then at the end of the day, white a nice long paragraph entry that talks about the day and how smoking is involved. Here's an example:

> Dear Journal,
> Here's a different spin on it and this may sound crazy but look at all the things I have to discipline myself to do just to be able to smoke. I have to go outside at nearly every establishment in the country just to have a cigarette. When I air travel, I have to go into those disgusting rooms that give me the impression of a jail cell (pun intended). I have to always have my car window down no matter what the weather because I'm a fresh air smoker and hate to be boxed in. I can't sit in my house and smoke because I will not burden my family, nor will I stink up my beautiful home. I always have to make sure I never run out of cigarettes, which is a real pain when we do things like go to the lake jet skiing. While doing this I have to find a way to keep them handy but keep them dry too. Then I always have to make sure I have a light. Then I have to find somewhere to smoke. How about that price? The taxation alone is enough to make

> me sick. I'll save well over $1200 a year just to stop. When I meet someone new, I try not to make it obvious that I smoke because I know it's a vice and I believe that they'll think less of me. I can't play basketball hard because I just get exhausted after 2 minutes. I would like to learn to whitewater kayak and it would be a big help if I were in decent shape and could hold my breath at least a little. I just can't see myself getting up when I'm 60 and hacking until I nearly puke. I've had people tell me that I don't look like a smoker and I don't really know what that means exactly, but I like to hear it anyhow.

This was a small clip out on my journal. Please don't take this step lightly. This is far more important than you realize, as well as a vital piece of this puzzle and its importance cannot be stressed enough.

10

The pen is mightier than the sword

What's the combination?

It takes many things working together to achieve a common goal. Like any combination lock where you need all the numbers, this is no different. Like the football team that has a great offense: If ten guys do their jobs and just one doesn't, they're in trouble. Apply the same concept her. If you are to succeed at quitting smoking, chances are that it won't be about any one thing that you did to finally succeed. It'll be about all the little things you do that are combined to achieve the product of success. I'm begging you to take every idea in these pages and just try them no matter how insignificant they may seem. You have absolutely nothing to loose and everything to gain.

Your wallet list

To some this may seem useless at first but I promise you this will make a difference (Remember I said it's the combination of many things). I made a list on a little post it note and kept it in my wallet 6 weeks before my quit date. Well, the truth is I didn't even have a quit date chosen yet, but I already had this list in my wallet. Mine included the following:

- I want to be a good roll model for my son.
- I absolutely HATE being controlled!
- Rising insurance costs for smokers: auto, home, health, life.

- Easily winded; stairs, swimming, playing with kids.
- It's very expensive; what could I do with that money?
- Get sick more; stay sick longer; that's more wasted money.
- Just the inconvenience infuriates me.

And here are more ideas for yours:

- Feel that I'm judged by non-smokers
- The after-smell on my clothes, furniture, car, house and everything.
- Not being able to breathe easily.
- Airport smoke rooms (Yuk!)
- The constant, nagging cough, headaches, occasional migraines.
- Lingering colds and bronchitis.
- Racing heartbeat, more sweating.
- Increased rate of hypertension.
- Dizziness after smoking too fast or too many cigarettes.
- Nausea from smoking too much.
- The constant coppery, ashy taste in my mouth.
- Yellow skin, teeth and fingernails.
- Scaly, unhealthy-feeling skin.
- Anxiety from the fear of what I was doing to myself, and the consequences.
- No relaxation, always feeling in need of something. A constant feeling of not being satisfied.
- Mini-withdrawals throughout the day.
- Cigarettes are like little thieves that steal time, life, money and freedom.
- Feelings of disgrace while spending time with non-smokers or excusing myself to go have a cigarette.

- Get less done due to the wasting of time while smoking.
- The late-evening/middle-of-the-night/snowing like crazy trip to the gas station.
- Going out in bad weather to smoke alone.
- Feelings of inadequacy because of the dependence.
- Driving my cat out of the room every time I lit up.
- Hiding it from your kids because you know it's wrong and you don't want them copying you.
- Dry mouth and foul breath all the time.
- Coughing so hard that I made myself sick.
- Cold hands and feet due to the constricted blood vessels.
- Fear of being unable to quit; and/or dying an untimely, painful death.
- The feeling of lack of oxygen when I tried to take a deeper or slower breath.
- Getting smoke in my eyes.
- Burning my lips on the filter.
- Occasionally burning my fingers
- Trying to light short butts, and feeling my eyebrows singe. Ouch!
- Re-lighting a previously torched cigarette, so I don't "waste" cigarettes.
- Overflowing ashtrays, ashes getting all over everything.
- Burn holes in my car upholstery, and on my clothes.
- It's only a matter of time until I fall asleep smoking.
- Eventually I will catch something on fire.
- Dry skin and chapped lips.
- The cost. All that money wasted on ruining my health and well-being.

- It fueled my compulsiveness relating to other bad habits, such as nail biting, and binge-eating.
- Having to reapply my lipstick after smoking.
- The filthy taste of cheap tobacco; brand names are so expensive.
- Having to crack the car window in the pouring rain, during a blizzard or just when it's nasty out.
- Tar build-up on windows, walls and furniture.
- The way my hair and skin smelled.
- Limited motivation and energy.
- Spilled tobacco in my purse, on my dresser, in my pockets.
- Lighting the filter end by mistake (yummy).
- Dropping a cigarette while driving.
- Trying to tap my ashes out the car window…while the window is rolled up.
- Dropping hot ashes or losing the tip of a cigarette.
- Oops! Tapped ashes in my drink.
- Feeling "exiled" in the smoking room (Yuk!).
- Dulled sense of taste and smell.

Add some of your own if you have more. That's a heck of a list with lots of reasons to quit. How many do you think you could come up with for not quitting smoking? I'll bet you'd be hard pressed to have even three.

Like I said, I made my list 6 weeks prior to quitting with no idea of when I would quit. Every single time I got money out of my wallet, I read it. Every single time I got a credit card out, I read it. When I got my Costco membership card out, I would step to the side, let others pass and read my list again. Sound neurotic? Well, all I know is it worked…it was part of the puzzle.

The 2-cent piece of paper

As long as we're on the subject of writing things down, let me throw this at you. Take a two-cent piece of paper and draw a line down the middle. On one side are the pros of quitting smoking (if there even are any); and the other put the cons. I actually still laugh at how effective something this primitive can be. I've been doing this for years and although I've made my share of stupid mistakes, not one of them was a result of this simple, yet incredibly effective method.

11

Wind for those sails

Online support groups

There are so many things online that will support you. Begin with something like a Yahoo Support Group, they're free and you not only get help and support, but also you can give help too. The comradery, acceptance and goodwill towards each other, even on a cyber level is heartwarming. The group I was on was my lifeline the first 3 weeks; I mean that literally. You can tell that the people genuinely care and every morning, rather than light up, I would go voice my frustration online. It made me feel better and it helped me go another morning without smoking. One thing to take note of: When I was 5 weeks smoke free, I actually said goodbye to everyone, and stopped posting because it made me think more about smoking than not and I had to cut that umbilical cord. I actually was doing so well it was a burden after I had made it over that hump…you may feel the same way.

Similarly, there's actual Quit Groups that you can join also for free. These are more like a club than a group. All they want is just a little information about you like age, length of time smoking, quit date estimate, and that's it. Surprisingly, they don't try to sell you anything and exist for the sole purpose of helping our smoking society with this challenge. They send you inspirational and informative emails every day in your mailbox. Some are stories about successes, others are people's quit date milestones. You may find a buddy that you can relate to and you may not, either way it's a good tool to help you.

Employee assistance

Most employers across the United States have programs set up people that want to quit do just that. If not, many Employers' Insurance will cover some type of program including smoking cessation prescriptions that can be very expensive. Companies aren't stupid and they recognize that healthier employees are better employees. Some other reasons are insurance cost are lower for non-smokers, energy level for non-smokers is higher, non-smokers are sick less. Check it out…it's worth the effort, you're worth the effort.

The never-ending

This is the information age where you can find anything you want on any subject if you have access to the Internet. You can tap into hundreds of thousands of hours of research, facts and figures, all there for the taking within minutes of logging on. If you need motivation, look for success stories that will inspire you. Or look for the person revealing the photos that show them recovering from having a lung removed. No, it's not morbid; it's reality and maybe fear will help you. Or look into just how the tobacco companies keep you on the hook by spending billions that you give them. You want to get livid, go to www.thetruth.com and soak it up. If that doesn't make you see red, I don't know what will.

Most cities of reasonable size have "smokers anonymous" groups and meetings. They cost little or nothing and you can meet people that are struggling with the same things you struggle with. There are also sometimes local groups in your area such as nicotine anonymous groups. If you check the local hospitals they usually have something like this. Look at the American Lung Association website too for additional information and phone numbers (all toll free).

Okay, you get the idea here. It's out there. What's out there? Well, pretty much anything and everything that you could possibly want or need to assist you and motivate you with this. Use it all to your advantage.

12

The Spiritual Side

The Universal Power

With the whole universe, the earth and all its wonders, all its mysteries and the absolute precision in which everything operates; it makes me wonder how anyone in their right mind can truly believe that life, all of life, all of creation is all just an accident? I will testify that I do believe in a living God and all that means nothing more than I'm a mere mortal just like you trying to make their way through this crazy world and help a few people in the process. It also means that I believe in a power that is as infinitely beautiful as it is powerful, and if you believe, know the power of prayer and also know that your knees are a good place to start this journey.

Faith vs. Fear; Hope vs. Doubt

Do you believe in things that you don't fully understand? Do you believe in good and evil? Can you see something even if it's not visible to the human eye? If you answered any one of these with a 'yes' then you understand that you have enemies that your eyes can't see, but can be seen (or felt if you prefer) by our heart. There is a human spirit within each of us that recognizes this evil but through rationalization, sometimes we dismiss it as coincidence, superstition or bad luck. There are forces out there that are for you, and there are others that are against you. Is the little man on your shoulder saying, "You can't quit. Why are you even bothering? You're just a looser. You don't have the discipline." Well, that's doubt my friend and I know this: Doubt is not from God, it's from His adversary. God is out there just like Satan is out there; and if you don't think that there's a spiritual war going on, well…think again.

So how to you beat doubt? Well, this is similar to the wish, want, need theory where wish = think, want = hope, and need = believe. It breaks down like this: First you start to 'think' that maybe you can do it. This is the wishful stage that has little substance or conviction but is a necessary predecessor to the second stage, which is the 'hope' stage. This is where you start pondering about if you did succeed, what would it be like? I would be free from those shackles, and how would it change things? Maybe I really could do this? Then you hit the final stage, the 'belief' stage. This is where you believe that you can and you start working towards that end by doing what you need to do. Once you believe in yourself, it's over. How about this for a thought: *What better gift to give God than to simply believe in ourselves.*

How dare you

On a personal note, I have been so blessed in my life so much more than I deserve. I am not wealthy nor have I had anything handed to me. However, I have an amazing wife of 14 years that I still love passionately, a happy and healthy son that wants for nothing, 3 dogs that fill in the boring spots, an awesome home in a beautiful neighborhood, a family in Western New York that I adore and many wonderful friends to share our joys with. I'm not a braggart and only told you that to tell you this: *With all the blessings that God has given me, I felt as if I was kicking Him right in the face every time I would light up.* Silly you think? Maybe, but I pictured that He was saying to me, "I give you all this, and this is how you treat your life; my most precious gift to you? How dare you?" It's definitely something to think about huh?

The Power or Prayer

The night before my quit day ("My Freedom Day" as I called it) I talked with God. Maybe this may seem irrelevant to some, but to me, and the struggle that I had with cigarettes, nothing could be any more relevant. I spilled my guts to God that evening before my first day as a non-smoker. I asked Him, no…I begged Him to help me get this taken care of. I prayed for His strength when I needed it. I'm a firm believer that if you need to ask God for something, one prayer from the heart will suffice. After all, He's God, which means He heard me, and He won't forget about me. And you know what? He listened and I will go to my grave saying that I'm convinced that He helped me through the rough times. I look back and it is oh so obvious, though I cannot explain it. The rough times weren't so rough and after 27 years, He's the only explanation. You'll just have to succeed, feel what I feel, and then you'll know for yourself.

Interestingly enough, I just knew that this was going to be the time that I made it. As amazing as it seems, I was right. In hindsight, there's no surprise. I talked with Him all the time while I was planning my quit date, but still smoking. I'd go for a walk around my work place, have a smoke and ask Him to help me be strong and that I was scared of failing again. He was with me…walking with me. I only prayed that one time asking for help with quitting and I never asked Him again. Oh sure I talked and prayed with Him before about the thought of it and what my concerns were but never spilled my emotional guts like that evening.

Person to Person

If you are a true believer, and chances are that you are, talk to Him about it. He helped me. I promise that He will help you too. The only catch: *You must fervently believe and cast out ANY seeds of doubt!* And yes, He'll help you but don't forget that it still takes effort. Another factor in determining your success is your attitude. This has to be an obsession at first. This means that, for about the first month, quitting has to the most important thing in the world to you. For just a month be fanatical about it until you get over a few mile markers. Please, read and internalize that last sentence again.

PART IV
The Divorce

13

The dissolution

It's been great but you're history!

Have you ever been guilty of this in a relationship: You know it's over. You're headed towards a dead end and you know it. There's nothing there but convenience. The love has gone elsewhere. But breaking up is rough. It's emotional. Someone always gets hurt. It just sucks having to do that. It means that someone has to move, and I don't want to go through that. It's just such a major pain so if we stick it out, maybe things will change and it will somehow magically heal themselves. But it never happens and eventually, all that bad stuff that you didn't want to happen…well, guess what, it happens anyhow. That's just life.

Okay now listen; I'm not trying to be a cold-hearted jerk here. And I do understand that families with kids can't just walk away without a fight because that happened to me and it was no fun. But let's face it, we've all done this in the past and more than likely we were too young to know better. However, I do have a theory that may make you chuckle: *"Smoking is like a lousy relationship. We hang on for years even though we're in misery and we know it's killing us."* Then when we finally cut that umbilical cord, finally draw that line in the sand, step over it, and it is only then that we realize that life just got a whole lot better and all it took was a little work.

Living without you

Why is it that we think that we can't live without that thing anyway? Just like the relationship I mentioned above, it's not that we can't; it's just uncharted territory. And just like that ending of that relationship, the first few weeks are going to be miserable. What in the human brain is more feared then the present situation? I'll tell you; the unknown. Sounds stupid but it's true. Think about it: Even with the thought of breaking up with someone, what are you asking yourself? What am I going to do at night? Who will I go to the movies with? Who will I go out to eat with? I'll have to go to the company Christmas party alone, what will I tell them? And on and on. Then as time goes by, none of those silly concerns matter anymore and eventually just fade away into nothingness. Well, guess what? Quitting smoking is the same thing. What I mean is that smoking is a relationship too; and one that you've had for years. Now with quitting on your mind you ask all the same types of questions. Check it out:

Question 1. What will I do after dinner without my favorite companion (the cigarette)?

Answer 1. How about relax and enjoy the company of your guests or your family.

Question 2. How am I going to live without my best buddy (the cigarette) in the morning with my coffee?

Answer 2. Get online and post a message on a support group rather than sucking toxic gases into your body. Change to gourmet coffee with the savings of not smoking. It tastes much better.

Question 3. I used to smoke and relax to kill time. What will I do when I'm bored without my buddy (the cigarette)?

Answer 3. How about not kill yourself just because you're bored. Go for a bike ride. Go take a shower. Go shoot hoops. Good Lord, do anything for Heaven's sake.

Question 4. What will I do at lunchtime and breaks during work without my faithful buddy (the cigarette)?

Answer 4. Walk around the block. If it's snowing, go watch the snowfall. If it's raining, go watch the rain. Enjoy the freedom. You have options; you're not being controlled now.

Question 5. What will I do because I used to love to smoke in bed right before I hit the sack?

Answer 5. How about curl up with a good book rather than smell up your bedroom and cause yellowish-orange stains on the ceiling.

So you see; it really is a relationship; part of your life. And it doesn't matter what you do during those times, it only matters what you don't do. Life without cigarettes is no different than breaking up with a girlfriend/boyfriend. You miss them badly for a few days and it hurts like hell. After a week, it's not so bad and it's getting better; slowly but surely the memories fade. After a month life is getting back to normal and you actually forget about them more often than not. After 6 months you'll kick yourself for not dumping them earlier because you're finally free from that emotional tyrant.

14

Onward and upward

Change of Life

No not menopause. When talking with my wife, Cassie, she told me about the success while on Weight Watchers, which opened my eyes to an interesting concept. What they are taught at Weight Watchers, at least her point of view on it, was that to loose weight and keep it off, you must change your lifestyle; you must change the way you think of food. Most people focus on eating less and that's their primary focus. My wife told me that for those that succeed as she did, they must learn to look at food differently. It's not for pleasure anymore but for nourishment and the sustenance of life. I know what you're thinking and no, that doesn't mean that you can't enjoy a plate of your favorite pasta, it's just that the perspective has changed. My wife used to wait all day and have no starches at all so when we went out to a nice Italian Restaurant, she could have all the pasta she wanted that night. It seems to me that it's like a reward system, similar to those that ex-smokers recommend. So, if I apply the same philosophy to quitting smoking then my chances at succeeding increase dramatically.

The non-choice

What is a non-choice? It's a subconscious action; one that you don't even think about. Understand that smoking is no longer a pleasure for you. You're addicted and you need to quit. But unfortunately, it's not just an addiction but also a way of life. Someone must change the way they look a cigarettes before quitting permanently can take place. Now, is the cigarette after dinner really necessary or is it simply and addiction? A habit? How about the one you have immediately upon rising in the morning? Is that the addiction? Or is it the habit? The answer it yes to all of it. The fact is you don't even think about it anymore; it's just something you do, right? That's why we say it's a way of life not just a bad habit. Have you ever caught yourself smoking and not even remember lighting it up? It's rhetorical, yes you have. Start looking at this as a different angle and you're on your way. Make in a conscious choice rather than a subconscious act and you're on your way. We'll talk about this more later.

Won't I get heavy?

Like I said, it's a way of life change not just a habit change. A concern for many smokers is the possibility of weight gain. Here are the facts: According to studies, the average smoker gains about 8 pounds after quitting. Here's another fact: I am 5'9" and was 165 pounds when I was smoking and I am now 173 pounds as a non-smoker, exactly 8 pounds. So I'd say that this is pretty accurate. However, weight gain isn't inevitable so let me tell you some facts before you go overboard. Your system slows down and you burn fewer calories but your body is also more efficient. Here's another fact: If you eat exactly the same diet after you quit, then you probably will gain a few pounds. I'm not a weight and health guru but all I can tell you what my wife said to me. She said "I'll take you a few pounds heavier over you being a smoker any day. Your breath doesn't stink anymore either." She then gave me a kiss and walked away. Again, do research on this and you'll find some fantastic information on what you can do to keep the weight gain to a minimum.

Some people are actually concerned that the little weight gain will hurt their health. I find this ludicrous after all, they've been inhaling toxins for the last umpteen years and now they're worried about this. The priorities these days kill me. The truth is the health risks of smoking outweigh the risks of gaining 5 to 10 pounds. Other than the fact that smoking causes more than 400,000 deaths each year in the United States, you would have to gain about 100 to 150 pounds after quitting to make your health risks as high as when you smoked. Read that last sentence again and tell me seriously, is this really a concern?

What to do

Exercise is an obvious way to help avoid gaining weight after you quit. Studies show that smokers have an easier time quitting when they add exercise to their smoking cessation plan. So pick something you love to do and do it as much as you can. It's a great outlet and reduces the stress of quitting.

Some people like to add something to their lives to fill the void they believe will be created by quitting. Exercise can help you control your weight and will help you commit to this new and healthier way of life. Personally, I really enjoyed those voids after the first week was over with. That's time that you give back to yourself. The older I get the more important time is. When you quit, that's a true gift and a major reward to yourself. I never thought I could sit in my garage and watch those awesome thunderstorms without a cigarette in my hand, but I do it now all the time and love it.

The best thing you can do to stay smoke-free is to prepare yourself long before your quit date. Plan exactly how you'll get through cravings by making a list of everything you can do when a craving hits. No I'm not going to give you a list. Make your own just for you. Hey, you might like to chop wood with an axe for all I know. My point is if you're going to plan for this, do it right the first time and get it done, but do it YOUR way.

Unorthodox works well

In about 2 minutes I could pull up 100 sites on the Internet that all tell you exactly what you should to do fight the cravings, but it's all generic. And since we already know that these will only work for a select few, let's try a different approach like make your own list of what to do. Sure, exercise can be an effective tool just like drinking lots of water, but being silly will work just as well. When the urge to smoke hits, try the following to break the pattern, then make up some of your own; the more bizarre the better in my opinion:

- Take a brisk10-minute walk on your break; look up at Heaven and talk to God. He's a great supporter, a wonderful conversationalist, and if you listen carefully, you'll hear Him.
- Do jumping jacks in back of the building at work. And I don't care who's watching.
- Go find somewhere to be alone. Now get on your knees and ask for strength.
- Suck on a lemon. Eat an apple. Brush and floss your teeth. For Heaven's sake, do anything.
- Go outside and scream at the tobacco companies; "YOU WILL NOT WIN THIS TIME! I WILL NOT BE CONTROLLED! YES, I'M A FREAK BUT YOU SUCK, AND YOU DON'T CONROL ME!" (I did this outside my work, and you cannot even imagine how many times I did it, but I said things that I cannot repeat here)
- Repeat the above suggestions again and add some of your own. Be weird and do off the wall stuff to break the patterns.

15

The right directions

All or nothing

Here's a question: Do you believe that the United States is the most non-committal society in the world? Makes you think doesn't it? Why is divorce so high? Why are Grandparents raising their own Grandkids? Hey, nobody's perfect but very few people know what it means to commit to something 100%. Yes I'm talking the 'do or die, no retreat; no surrender' attitude where giving in isn't even an alternative. What people don't understand is that 99% committed is still 100% uncommitted. Some people won't agree so let's look at it this way: If you're married, and you're spouse is faithful to you 99% of the time, is that okay with you? Of course not because they're still 100% unfaithful, right? Exactly! You're either committed or you're not. There is no sitting on the fence here.

Danger ahead

Indecision is still a decision. Here's the scenario: Hey, I'm going to get an ice cream; you want one? It's either yes or no. If it's yes, fine. If it's no, fine. If it's 'I don't know', then it's still no. This is not a difficult concept to grasp although I see this happen to people every day concerning everything from what to have for dinner, to which mini van to buy. It's real simple; if you don't know if you can commit, I mean totally 100%, to the decision of quitting smoking, then wait until you're ready. Okay, am I telling you not to quit? No or course not! But hear me out: You're reading this for one of two reasons: (1) You're either ready right now or (2) You're searching for the tools, motivation and education to succeed because you know it's getting close. Honestly, when I was smoking, I had so many people hounding me to quit and I just wanted them to leave me the hell alone! You know why? Because I wasn't ready yet; and I knew that but they didn't. When I was ready I got it done. Now it's your turn.

Point of no return

My son and I love to ride ATVs. We live in Northern Nevada and where we go riding there are many hills that just call out to us. It is such a thrill to take on a big climb but there is a certain amount of danger. And although neither one of us are experts by any means, we do know this: The one rule of climbing any decent hill when on an ATV that can be deadly to break is that you don't stop once you start that climb…period! You absolutely cannot for any reason, with the only exception being mechanical failure, change your mind in the middle of that climb. If you commit to taking on a 45-degree hill that's 200 feet high, you had better stay on the throttle until you're at the top! There are no other options at that point without serious consequences. If you stop, you're probably going to get hurt, possibly quite seriously. And although this may be a totally different subject that we're talking about here, but theory applies when there is a commitment involved.

Okay, my point is this: Concerning the task of quitting smoking, if you can get yourself, mentally, to the point of no return, the point where you are not giving in no matter what life throws at you, no matter what doubts Satan tries to put in you. You'll beat your head against a solid walnut door before you smoke; you'll turn away from your friends if they don't support you, you'll scrap with someone if they put you down, or you'll yell at a tree if your boss is a jerk (don't get fired by yelling at him/her). When you recognize that characteristic in yourself, you won't fail. There's just no way.

Control freaks

The U.S. Marines teach "Death before Dishonor." The Marines teach discipline probably more than any other military branch, with the Navy Seals being the only comparable group. Why? Because when our soldiers are on the front line going to battle, their superiors need to KNOW that they will not hesitate. They have complete control over those soldiers because of their training. I know it sucks, but if they die in battle it's because of what they're taught; Death before Dishonor. I will say that I for one appreciate all our freedoms that they've provided for my family and me but my point is this: They are literally controlled by that Commanding Officer.

Now think of this: Have you ever met a smoker that you just know will die on a breathing machine with a cigarette in their mouth? I've met people that regardless of what they know, what they hear, how badly they cough and hack, no matter if they can't even climb one lousy flight of stairs; you absolutely know they will never even consider trying to stop. Now, think about the control that cigarettes have over this person. Just like the scenario about the soldiers, that cigarette has that much power over smokers as that Commanding Officer does over those Marines, and I think that's just sad. The soldier dies for a reason; the smoker dies for no other reason that to make some idiot rich. I guess they have their own Death before Dishonor loyalty for their cigarettes. They would literally rather die than quit. They fear it that much! That was huge for me when I quit because they had control of me, and I hated being controlled more then anything. Are you controlled? Probably not to that extreme but you definitely are controlled to a large degree. Aren't you sick of it? I hope so.

16

Just a little odd

Going…going…gone!

People think I'm in la-la land all the time. Well, except my wife. Why? Because I talk to myself while I walk, work, write, mow my lawn and just about every other thing I do. It just helps sometimes. It helps clear your head and it can help when trying to solve a problem. Albert Einstein once said that only above average intelligence people talk to them selves. And although I don't know if that's true, I'm not hurting anybody so who cares. I truly believe in the power of the tongue and I can promise you that there is a lot of power in speaking things. I heard a very wise man say; "The voice is the gateway to your inner ear, then it enters your soul. Use it wisely."

Okay, to some this is just going to seem ridiculous. You'll laugh at this, but before I quit, hundreds of people saw me talking away (with no passenger) in my car and knew I was nuts. But every single day for my first 2 weeks of being smoke free, as well as 3 weeks prior, on my 50-minute drive home from work, I talked with an imaginary friend in my passenger seat the whole way. I told him how proud of myself I was, all the benefits of my decision, how I felt like I've been freed, how it didn't bother me not having a smoke, how much better I felt, etc. And you know what? It worked and that's all I cared about. It was part of that combination I talked about earlier. And at the same time, it helped me forget about how badly I wanted a cigarette. In addition, at least for me, this method, speaking the past tense, like I had already succeeded, will help solidify the belief in myself that you can beat this once and for all.

Togetherness

I believe that self-talk, belief and mental toughness go together as well as the Father, Son and the Holy Ghost. Okay, maybe not that extreme but the point is this: Mental toughness can be accredited to just being stubborn. And to a certain point so can belief, but self-talk is what changes your subconscious mind. That part of your brain that says, "I know what you're doing and sorry but, it isn't working."

Break the chain

You need to set a quit date. I read the 'experts', you know the Stanford guys, who say set it for 2 weeks out. Again, sorry college boys but I set mine for 4 ½ weeks out and I succeeded. See, I told you before; do what YOU need to do…not what they say, because they don't have the first clue.

I called my quit day my "Freedom Day" and there is no standard. The word quit still scared me at the time. Hey whatever works right? Calling it the "quit day" still freaks out some people. So you can call is whatever you like. It seems that some folks are intimidated by the words because they feel they're loosing something. How about one of these:

- My Re-Birth Day
- My Day of Triumph
- My Self-Reunion Day
- My Day of Reckoning
- My Judgment Day
- My Victory Day
- My Inauguration
- My Breakout Day
- My Day of Liberation
- My Independence Day

- My Freedom Day
- My Day of Supremacy

These may sound ridiculous to you but it really has to mean something. If you don't like these find something that fits your personality and don't let it go. When I talk about the day I quit smoking, umpteen years later, I still say that May 6th was my "Freedom Day." Not once have I ever, and I mean ever, referred to it as my quit day. I'm telling you, the little things count big.

Remember there are no rules for this endeavor; no standards. I once heard this: "Thinking outside the box is creative, but realizing that there is no box is ingenious." And I'll never forget it.

PART V
Staying Single

17

Maintain your distance

Good One

I don't like sarcasm unless it's meaningful, but it also cannot deliberately hurt someone. I saw this on the back window of a van in big bold letters: "Satan's a pimp, don't be his ho!" And although this may be a bit extreme, but it's still accurate…at least to me. The funniest part of this is that a few weeks later, just by coincidence, I met the owner of that van at a friends' daughter's birthday party. He was a minister from the town I live in and he's anything but extreme. I talked with him about it, because personally I think it's awesome. All he said was this; "I'm just trying to make a point, that's all." He was just a preacher with a soft-spoken attitude and I loved it!

So here's the thing: Aren't the tobacco companies all just pimps? Then what are the smokers? Are they the hoes? Here's an analogy: The pimps, (opps, I mean the tobacco companies) make all the money while the hoes (opps again, I mean the smokers) are out taking all the risks of illnesses and death (liver disease, cancer, emphysema, etc.). The pimps (tobacco companies) go home and sleep at night, in their nice cozy beds, and the smokers (hoes) are out whoring around making money for the pimps (tobacco companies) running to the store getting a smoke because they ran out. Is this silly? I may be strange but you cannot tell me it's not accurate. Anyway, you get my point.

Got attitude? If not, get one!

I do not judge smokers and I never will. How could I? I smoked for 27 years. However, I was one of those rare types that actually cared about the well being of the non-smokers around me. I never smoked in my car if my passenger was a non-smoker. I was always considerate and would put out my cigarette if it was truly bothering someone. In restaurants I rarely smoked and if I did, I made sure it didn't interfere with the smoke free people enjoying their meal. The good news is this: There are some of those types of smokers out there. Now the bad news: It's doubtful that you will ever encounter one. Seriously, when you finally beat this thing, stick up for yourself. You will work your rear off and go through hell to succeed at quitting. So when you're finally smoke-free, don't you dare let someone smoke in a non-smoking section on a restaurant you're in if it's bothering you. Now let's not get stupid here. If it's a 315-pound biker, let the management handle it, but you get the idea. Now let's face it, if you're at a sports bar watching football, you're going to breathe lots of smoke so just sit where there's good ventilation, away from the smokers. If it's too much, leave if you have to. Especially if you're thinking that you might relapse. You are much more important that a lousy football game or any other sport.

Get physical

No not the song. The issue here is about you staying single and as far away as possible from that old friend that was killing you. I've had people ask me, "Will I really feel better in just a week or two?" I tell them yes I vow to you that you will! I was getting winded just going up my stairs when going to bed at night. As a matter of fact, that's what prompted me to get serious about my quest to be smoke free. I don't get winded anymore going upstairs. When I go swimming with my family, I can actually do 7 laps in a 25 meter pool before I'm got winded. Before quitting it was only 2 laps and I was done and would have to stop (this is not an exaggeration). That's pretty bad for someone that was once on the swim team at school. You will hack up some stuff initially, but within a week or two, your wheezing will stop and you will feel a tremendous difference.

Have some fun already!

You can go find lists on the Internet that are as long as your arm on what to do so there's really no need for me to list them here for you. Physical activity helps but is not a cure all. In my humble opinion, you must do things that you like to do. If you hate to swim, please don't swim in an effort to aid you in your smoke free lifestyle. Personally, I love to shoot hoops. After I quit smoking, I shot basketball with my son or by myself every single day for the first 3 months after work…I mean literally every single day after I got home from work for about an hour. I swam occasionally but we usually just ended up shooting hoops there too (they have a floating basketball hoop). I always keep my yard nice so that's not so much enjoyable as it is necessary. I'm spoiled and have toys to keep me busy on the weekends and I know that not everybody is that fortunate, but there's always something to do; whether it's cleaning the machines or even just sitting in the shade and listening to the breeze move through the leaves on the trees. It's amazing how you can just sit alone and relax; knowing that this void of time can be cherished rather than be ruined by the need for a cigarette. Heck, if you live by a river, go sit at its banks; it's therapeutic. Start planning what you're going to do with the $1200 a year that you're not spending on cigarettes. Enjoy your new lifestyle because what you will have accomplished is a beautiful thing.

Look, you get the picture here. You know what you like to do and now you'll get to do it longer, with more vitality, and with much less effort. How cool is that?

18

What's in it for me?

Reward yourself

I cannot tell you how critical this is and it doesn't matter how insignificant it may seem. I don't care if it's something as simple as treating yourself to an ice cream cone of your favorite flavor. Anything I have ever read about any type of self improvement course supports this idea. Furthermore, anyone in any field that involves a goal of any kind as well as anyone I have ever talked to personally concerning kicking this habit, or any other habit for that matter, says this is a great idea and I endorse it as well. Why? Because it worked.

Think of something that you've been putting off buying, not necessarily because you can't afford it, but because you always find something more practical to do with the money. It may be a music CD, which was one of my first rewards. For the ladies it may be a new style of bathing suit. Possibly you would like to buy a movie to add to your home collection, or a night out at favorite restaurant. How about an afternoon at a day spa? Maybe you want to stash the money, which is something I did until I had $300 saved up, then I went and totally blew it without so much of a hint of guilt…and my awesome wife backed me the whole way on it! You get the picture here. There are a thousand things that you can do for yourself.

My first book that I had published, *Dancing With Angels*, was almost entirely paid for with cigarette money that I was stashing. Become a master at stashing money for yourself when you kick this, then treat yourself. You will have earned it, and you'll deserve it.

Master of illusions

However, rewards are not always necessarily things that can be purchased with money. There are some elusive rewards are pretty awesome; the ones that we really don't pay attention to, the ones you can't see. I have never traveled as a non-smoker…ever! I don't travel that much; I like my domicile, however my son and I were going to New York to visit my family and we were going through Atlanta. We had a 3-hour layover and we had a blast walking around, eating and relaxing between flights and I didn't have to worry about having a cigarette. What a difference that simple thing made in the enjoyment part of traveling. Maybe it would feel great to not always feel out of place since 79% of the adult population doesn't smoke. I now enjoy walking outside in the morning and smelling the flowers that are about 20 feet from my front door. I never smelled them before but now my senses have improved dramatically, and it's a real treat. How do you think I feel having my wife tell me that she likes kissing me now because my breath doesn't stink like before when I was smoking? That meant more to me than words can say.

Different angle

Then there are some of the inconveniences that you've never really thought about because as a smoker, you just accept them. Think about these: You don't have to go outside when it's snowing and freeze your rear off just to have a smoke anymore. You won't have to worry about little burn holes in you car seats or in your clothes because a hot ash falls accidentally. Beside the ashes get everywhere. I liked that I could drive and relax with the air conditioner on rather than have the windows down when it's 100 degrees outside because as I said, I was a fresh air smoker and hated to be boxed in. And how about the time that you will have free to do whatever you wish. This one will scare you at first because you'll initially think that you need to fill that time or go crazy thinking about smoking. But when you've made it and you're a non-smoker, I promise you that this one is priceless. Another will be no more hiding this from anyone like people that look up to us. My son was a big one for me. Then when I succeeded he was running around telling everybody. How could I relapse after that? Now that's motivation.

Plan ahead

So, what are you going to do for yourself at 1 week, 2 weeks, a month, two months and so on? Figure it out now before you ever even get started. Plan now, plan ahead so you're ready. In your quit smoking journal (that you've already gotten right?), make a list of all the things that you want to do with your cigarette money. Don't judge and just write anything that comes to mind. You can go over them later when you need the motivation, and then put a time line on when you're going to have the ones that mean a lot to you. Please don't skip doing this. If you simply let the money you're saving get absorbed into every day life, you will be missing out on a major weapon on this fight for your freedom. It will also diminish somewhat. Don't to that, it's not fair to you.

19

Take the high road

Flirtin' with disaster

The forks in the road of life are the moments where you're tested. Your faithfulness to your spouse will be tested on occasion. Your loyalty to a friend will be tested when someone bad mouths them behind their back. Will you speak up or play along? Will you drive a car when you know that you've probably had one drink too many. These are all forks in the road of life. And if we take the wrong one, it may change the rest of your life…literally.

I've seen it at least 20 times and it always ends up the same. He's out with friends. Many of them smoke. He's been clean for 4 months. He's had a few drinks then he starts rationalizing: I can have a smoke…I'll be fine. The next morning he either has a pack on his nightstand, or he's going to get one. Every single time this happens! You are no different and if you try too prove me wrong, you're just going to prove me right. Please listen to a 27 year smoker: NOT EVEN ONE…NOT EVEN ONT DRAG! Do not sabotage all the work that you've put into this, and if you are yet to begin, remember this well. Please understand that this is coming from a 27-year smoker. I've done it a half dozen times, trust me on this one. Ask any recovering alcoholic, cocaine addict, compulsive gambler or anyone else that's recovering from a serious addiction and they'll tell you the same thing; that they are one action away from being completely addicted and out of control again. Just recognize the truth that quitting cigarettes is no different.

Choices…it's all choices.

No matter what else, one thing that you'll always have to accept is that it's your choice. Just like the fork in the road, you've got to make a choice and take full responsibility for that choice. Every single time you light up it's another choice. No matter how many billions they spend on advertising, it's still your choice. Nothing matters other than the choices you make and if you choose to have another smoke and say, "I can't quit yet, maybe the first of the year" then you just gave that much more time and control away, but you chose to do it. Have you ever heard this line: How come if you kill a person you're a murderer; but if you kill a million then you're a conqueror? Well, they're not murdering, they're conquering but the tune of hundreds of thousands a year. Legally, at least by man's laws and they will continue to do so as long as people buy their product. If someone asked you to play Russian roulette with a 6-shooter if he gave you $10,000, would you? How about $100,000? Some people would and those are the people that have a whole lot more guts (I think I mean stupidity) than I do. Think about this for a minute: Which cigarette is the one that's going to cause that first cell of lung cancer? Is it the next one, or maybe it'll be 200 cigarettes down the road, or maybe 2000. How about the one that's going to ruin your liver? How about the one that your son or daughter sees in your mouth, when they finally say to themselves, "If he does it, why can't I?" Getting a little uncomfortable? Good because you need to focus on the things that are important. Either way, your choices make you what you are in life. Remember that the choices you make today are the choices you have to live with for the next 1 to 10 years. I'm only 45 but I've figured out that when we make choices, whether good or bad, we live with them for a very, very long time. I've also learned that making the right choice is usually, if not always the more difficult one.

Every time I bought a pack of smokes for about 2 years prior to quitting, I thought about it and knew that I was making a lousy choice. Do you feel that way? I finally made the decision when someone that I don't know very well, but am acquainted with was diagnosed with bladder cancer. Yes, he was a smoker and although the doctor couldn't prove that it caused it, he made it clear that he thought is was. When did he finally choose to quit? About 3 weeks after the initial diagnosis. He's doing well now with and there appears to be no cancerous tissues left after 2 minor surgeries…and yes he's still smoke free. Amen, another victory!

Accept the "or else"

You remember Mom saying to you "you'd better do what I ask you, or else!" So just understand that there are only two things that can happen at this fork in your road: (1) You quit and the quality of your life will improve overall or (2) You don't quit in which case accept the consequences that could be quite frightening. If you're okay with number (2) then you must be willing to accept the "or else" or the consequences. There is no sitting on the fence here; no in betweens. This is a fork in your road.

Just understand that the consequences of our actions are our rewards or punishment. You can tell how well your decision making was in the last year or two just by looking at your situations and circumstances of today. And the decisions you make today, that is which fork in the road that you take right now; will result in the joy or the despair that you experience in the near and distant future.

20

Finally, let's clear the air

Here are the top 15 questions/statements that I've either heard or read that I believe need answering. Some are relevant and some are just controversial. There are hundreds of these but I am going to cover the ones that I believe are the most important (from a smoker's perspective because I was one) and hopefully that will help you be informed. I would have loved to have someone to answer some or all of these for me. Most of the myths out there are just garbage but some are valid….sort of. You need to know where you stand either way.

1.) I've tried before and failed. I don't have the will power to quit
First let me tell you that 'will power' is an over used buzzword used by the very people that try to get everyone addicted to their lousy stinking poison. It does NOT take will power to quit smoking. It takes many things, usually a combination of things including some emotion, but here are just a few: tenacity, faith in self, planning, being informed, commitment, and my favorite…stubbornness. As far as the 'I quit before and it didn't work' syndrome, well, that's just an excuse so don't go there with me…I won't let you. Very few people ever quit on their first attempt although it can be done. It's possible that you very well could be one of those first time success stories. Here's the truth: Of those people that eventually succeed at quitting smoking, it takes them 3 or 4 times before they finally succeed for good. Knowledge is part of your arsenal…be informed!

2.) I've heard that cessation is the best way to quit because it's easier, but aren't they expensive?
Okay this is just ludicrous. How much do you spend a year on smokes? Even if you only smoke a half a pack a day, it's still around $600 a year. There isn't a cessation program out there that will cost anywhere near that much unless you're getting taken for a ride. Now the next issue: Smoking cessation programs are wonderful for some, and not for others. Personally, I think it's hard enough putting your body though a major change like this without putting yet more crap into our body. That's a personal choice you will have to make. Research, research and research some more.

3.) What is this Hell Day that everyone talks about?
Let me explain Hell Day. It's the worst day that you will have while quitting and you'll want a cigarette from the time you wake up until the time you go to bed. You'll want to hurt somebody or something the whole day. My Hell Day was day 5. It'll most likely be in the first week. I was at work when I had mine, and I was nearly in was tears the whole day. And yes, I did cry a bit, mostly from anger. The only thing that kept me going is thinking about what I had allowed the tobacco companies to do to me, and I was going to beat those bastards! I'm pleading; no I'm begging you not to let this deter you from quitting. You're not going to die, but you sure will be tested. If you know it's coming, that's half the battle.

4.) How will I even get through one day without thinking about cigarettes?
I'll be honest here and say that I used to think the same thing. At first I got excited about just not having one. Then it got to where I would notice that I forgot all about the morning cigarette, or whichever cigarette. And I remember the first day that I did not think about a cigarette the whole day at work (just from 9 to 5); it was May 25th, 19 days after quitting. It took over 8 weeks of being smoke free to forget about it for a whole 24 hour period. You'll notice it's just stepping stones; and it really is very exciting. When I realized that I forgot to have a smoke for a whole day, I was running around telling everyone. They may have though I was nuts but I didn't care. Pay attention to the little things because over the course of

time, all those little changes start to exponentially grow and the result is beautiful.

5.) I've smoked so long the damage is irreparable; why bother?
Okay this is not even an intelligent statement, although I've heard it several times from seemingly intelligent people. The truth is we all know that, with the exception of having a cancer in your body that's spreading, the body does heal itself. Again, the Internet has all the free information you will ever need on any subject. When I was in the middle of my quitting battle, I could rattle off more statistical facts than most doctors; and some people may have mistaken me for the head of the American Cancer Society. Again, the information is out there, so be informed.

6.) Lite cigarettes are better for you right?
This isn't really worth a lot of time. And to think that lite cigarettes are healthier, well that's just ludicrous. Studies have proven that you will smoke more, take in more when you smoke them, and inhale deeper. It's proven. I'm not an expert but that sounds like they'd be worse for you if anything.

7.) Shouldn't I keep a pack of cigarettes in the freezer so I don't feel helpless?
I don't recommend this. Although it works for a select few, I have only met one person in my life that did it this way successfully. That's some pretty lousy odds…enough said.

8.) I like smoking. I can quit if I want to.
Do not be deceived my friend. There's a lot of rationalizing going on when there is an addiction involved. Hey, there's a word I haven't used much…a*ddiction*. I don't like the word because one of the meanings for it is this: "Dependence or practice that is beyond one's control." The reason I don't like it is that I don't believe that's true. The definition says that it's "beyond one's control." Well, that's crap! If it weren't than how did I quit? Conversely, habit is defined as "A recurrent, often unconscious pattern of behavior that is acquired through frequent repetition." Okay, now, studies have proven that after 72 hours addictive substances are gone from your

system. So, all that remains then is the habit, the psychological and physiological elements, which can be undone by simply replacing those behaviors with constructive behaviors. All that just to say one thing; it's just going to take a little effort and some good choices.

9.) I like to drink socially. How can I ever do that without a cigarette?
This is probably part of my stubborn Italian side in me, but I never gave up my coffee, my Bacardi Coolers or the occasional shot of bourbon with friends while my team is winning. I just wanted to quit smoking…not everything else. You may have to make some adjustments but that's okay. I told you that rather than have my coffee in the morning with a smoke, I'd share my thoughts on the online support site instead. It worked and I still enjoy my freshly ground Starbucks to this day. My point is to make your own adjustments to your routines that you can live with and if you have to stop having coffee for a month it won't kill you, but smoking may.

10.) Does it really promote gum disease?
I just had to put this is here and I'll tell you why: When I had my first dentist visit after I quit, I had been smoke free for 4 months. After Vicki, my hygienist, was done, she said see how much easier that was. I asked her why and she said that the tar from the cigarette smoke sticks to the teeth, and the plaque sticks to the tar stains much easier than just your tooth without the film of tar. With God as my witness, that was the first cleaning I've had in about 7 years, maybe more, that she didn't have to use that gel that numbs your gum area. Sorry to be so petty and simplistic…but that fired me up.

11.) Will I really feel better in just a week?
Yes I swear to you that you will! I was getting winded just going up my stairs when going to bed at night. As a matter of fact, that was one of the things that prompted me to get serious about my quest to be smoke free. I don't get winded anymore going upstairs. When I go swimming with my family, I can actually do 7–10 laps in a 25-meter pool before I'm got winded. Before quitting, 2 laps forced me to stop and I was gasping for air (this is not an exaggeration). That's pretty bad for someone that was once

on the swim team at school. You will hack up some stuff initially, but within a week or two, your wheezing will stop and you will feel a tremendous difference.

12.) They're part of my life; how can it live without them?
They're not part of your life; they control your life! For me, this was one of my biggest motivators. I read a great story about a successful quitter: He was out of town on business, at his hotel with no rental car and he was out of cigarettes. It was pouring rain outside so he figured he had no choice so he started walking down to the corner market a block away. He got half way there, he was drenched with no umbrella, and he looked up to Heaven then yelled, "I get the point." He turned around, went back to the hotel, got dried off and cleaned up and never smoked again. Although I cannot remember where I read this I do remember that it was a true story. It has stuck with me for years and still makes me chuckle. The power of an emotional decision is awesome.

13.) Will I have a hard time sleeping at first?
Yes, probably. This was a complete surprise to me. I had many sleepless nights in the bedroom for the first 2 or 3 weeks. Well, not really sleepless, just a lot of tossing and turning. This was a very strange feeling because it didn't happen until about 3 days into my quit. Normally I'm one of those people that could sleep through an earthquake. But because my body was without something it craved, I would wake up 3 or 4 times a night out of a dead sleep, I'd go get a drink of water or whatever, then go back to sleep if I could. There was a few nights that I watched some late television and actually slept in the recliner in front of the television. Oh well, what ever worked. You really can't battle this from what I can tell, but I always had a bottle of non-prescription sleep aid pills to help me if needed them. I used them to help me sleep a few nights a week, but only for a few weeks, and then just weaned myself off them when I was sleeping better.

14.) Do you really get all bound up after quitting?
Some do; some don't. This may make you chuckle initially, but after quitting, I could not have a good bowel movement for the life of me. I have

talked with others that had the same problem. You may think that's strange but, unfortunately it can be part if quitting so it's only fair that I tell you. Anyhow, just adjust your diet accordingly to help you in this area. It lasted me about a 3 weeks and this, for me personally, was nearly as bad as the cravings. Like I said, add some fiber to your diet and you'll be fine.

15.) Should I chain smoke like the dickens right before I quit?
I've had people ask me this and I must look at them like they have two heads. This is just insane. That's like saying, "I saw that her passenger door was ajar so I side-swiped her on the Highway, while were both doing 65 mph, in an effort to close it for her." It's like this: Duh? Why would anyone do this? Why would you fill your body with more nicotine and poison just because you're going to quit soon? It just makes no sense to me.

PART VI
(TCM) Time Compartment Management

21

How TCM works

This isn't exactly Nuclear Physics here but rather quite a simple concept. I did a little jaunt in the U.S. Navy back in the early 80s. One thing I learned is that the reason the U.S. Navy vessels are so difficult to sink is because of something called compartmentation. There are thousands of tiny compartments all over those ships and they're all sealed with water-tight doors. For example, if that vessel's hull gets penetrated at compartment number A-321, then all that needs to be done to save the ship is to close off that compartment thereby keeping the rest of the ship from taking in water. This is a simple design that the engineers of the Titanic unfortunately missed.

So, if those monster ships can be kept safe simply by carefully managing all those little compartments, then why couldn't I better control my time, life and habits by monitoring all my *compartments of time* each day? We live our lives in little compartments of time. For instance, we have the one compartment when we have our coffee in them morning, then another is the shower, then another is eating breakfast and another is driving to work. All these little bits of time make up our day. Now, if we simply keep a watchful eye on them, write down what we're doing, you will be amazed at how easily you can change behavioral patterns, like smoking.

I usually wake at 0600, and usually hit the sack around 2200 or 10 PM. Now, if I break my day up into 30-minute time compartments I will have 33 of them if I count the 0600 one. Now with a graph that shows my compartments of time, then I can visualize what my day is like while I smoke through this simple method. And if I can visually see it, I can start to envision what I need to do to change some things. For instance, if I asked someone, "When do you smoke," their answer may be something like, "Whenever I feel like it" or "I have no idea?" But there also would be those specific times like "right after lunch" or "when I'm on the freeway going home." When you use this method, you can actually see it; thereby you can change your behavior through conscious steps that will help you feel like you have more control.

On the following page is an example of a Time Compartment Management (TCM) graph for a typical workday; with the X's representing cigarettes smoked. By visually monitoring the compartments of time, you can actually see when you smoke and it becomes much more controllable to change patterns, particularly those that are done unconsciously. This represents the log book I spoke of earlier and of course this works in conjunction with your journal. Both the graph and the journal are of equally high importance here. On the sample graph we have Day 1 and Day 2. Notice how the days look pretty much the same except and by just making a few minor changes you went from smoking 22 cigarettes n Day 1, to only 15 in Day 2! And all we did was be observant and pay attention.

How TCM works 93

Time	Time Compartment No. (TC)	Day 1	Day 2
6:00	1	X	X
6:30	2		
7:00	3	X	X
7:30	4		
8:00	5	X	X
8:30	6	XX	X
9:00	7		
9:30	8	X	X
10:00	9		
10:30	10		
11:00	11	XX	X
11:30	12		
12:00	13		
12:30	14	X	X
13:00	15	XX	X
13:30	16		
14:00	17		
14:30	18		
15:00	19	XX	X
15:30	20		
16:00	21	X	
16:30	22		
17:00	23	XX	X
17:30	24		
18:00	25	X	X
18:30	26		

19:00	27	X	X
19:30	28		
20:00	29	X	X
20:30	30		
21:00	31	X	X
21:30	32	X	X
22:00	33	X	

Above is an example of TCM graph for the average smoker (1 pack a day) and some ideas for possible pattern changes.

1. Okay, look at TC 6 above. We don't need two cigarettes in a row, cut one out.

2. Look at TC 11. Don't have two again. Just have one.

3. Look at TC 15. Again, just have one and cut the other one out.

4. Look at TC 21. Challenge yourself. Cut this one out.

5. Another double at TC 23. It's not necessary, cut one out.

How TCM works 95

For heavier smokers, simply make more time slots because you smoke more frequently.

Time	Compartment No.	Day 1	Day 2
6:00	1	X	X
6:15	2		
6:30	3	XX	X
6:45	4		
7:00	5	X	XX
7:15	6	X	X
7:30	7		
7:45	8	XX	X
8:00	9	X	X
8:15	10		
8:30	11	X	
8:45	12	X	XX
9:00	13		
9:15	14		X
9:30	15		
9:45	16	XX	X
10:00	17		
10:15	18	X	X
10:30	19		
10:45	20	X	X
11:00	21		
11:15	22	X	X
11:30	23		
11:45	24	X	X
12:00	25		

12:15	26	X	X
12:30	27	XX	X
12:45	28		
13:00	29	X	X
13:15	30	X	
13:30	31		
13:45	32	XX	X

Above is an example of TCM graph for a heavy smoker (about 2 packs a day) along with some ideas on possible pattern changes. Simple, you get the idea here.

Sorry to be so simplistic. I know there's nothing magical here but understand that just becoming consciously aware of your actions is half the battle. I used to have a cigarette just before work, whether I just had one 15 minutes prior or not; and whether I really wanted one or not. It made no sense when I started looking at my TCM graph. And the list goes on and on; so will yours. You'll be amazed to discover how many times a you light one up when you don't even really want one; or could care less if you had one or not, where maybe you were just killing time or were bored.

You get the idea though. Like I said, no physics here, just a little time management that'll help us give some quality time back to you so you're not so controlled. From my own experience, and using this simple method, I got down to 10 cigarettes a day just before I quit and all I did was inventory what I was doing…that's all. Why did I do this? Because that way I didn't feel like it was such an enormous emotional leap to quit. If you think that would help your psyche then do it as well. The only reasoning behind this is that you get to where you're only smoking when you actually want one, rather than going through the thoughtless motions and in doing so, you can literally cut down to between 25% and 40% like I mentioned earlier. The amazing part is all you have to do to achieve these results is simply inventory what you're doing through the TCM graph, and commit to it, that's it.

Use the TCM method in addition to your journal (a simple notebook will do) and just commit to them both. You already started writing in your journal right? If not please go get one right now and begin. Sometimes that's the hardest part, just beginning. Then take it with you everywhere you go.

At the end of this chapter there is 30 days worth of TCM sheets for both average (1 pack a day) and heavy smokers (2 packs a day). You can either use the ones I've provided or create and print your own from Microsoft Excel. If you don't have a computer, draw lines down a piece of lines paper and write everything in. Commit and follow through.

Time Compartment Management Graph—Average Smoker
Page 1 of 5

Time	Time Compartment No. (TC)	Day 1	Day 2	Day 3	Day 4	Day 5	Day 6
6:00	1						
6:30	2						
7:00	3						
7:30	4						
8:00	5						
8:30	6						
9:00	7						
9:30	8						
10:00	9						
10:30	10						
11:00	11						
11:30	12						
12:00	13						
12:30	14						
13:00	15						
13:30	16						
14:00	17						
14:30	18						
15:00	19						
15:30	20						
16:00	21						
16:30	22						
17:00	23						
17:30	24						
18:00	25						

Time Compartment Management Graph—Average Smoker
Page 1 of 5 (Continued)

18:30	26	
19:00	27	
19:30	28	
20:00	29	
20:30	30	
21:00	31	
21:30	32	
22:00	33	

Time Compartment Management Graph—Average Smoker
Page 2 of 5

Time	Time Compart-ment No. (TC)	Day 7	Day 8	Day 9	Day 10	Day 11	Day 12
6:00	1						
6:30	2						
7:00	3						
7:30	4						
8:00	5						
8:30	6						
9:00	7						
9:30	8						
10:00	9						
10:30	10						
11:00	11						
11:30	12						
12:00	13						
12:30	14						
13:00	15						
13:30	16						
14:00	17						
14:30	18						
15:00	19						
15:30	20						
16:00	21						
16:30	22						
17:00	23						
17:30	24						
18:00	25						

Time Compartment Management Graph—Average Smoker
Page 2 of 5 (Continued)

18:30	26
19:00	27
19:30	28
20:00	29
20:30	30
21:00	31
21:30	32
22:00	33

Time Compartment Management Graph—Average Smoker
Page 3 of 5

Time	Time Compartment No. (TC)	Day 13	Day 14	Day 15	Day 16	Day 17	Day 18
6:00	1						
6:30	2						
7:00	3						
7:30	4						
8:00	5						
8:30	6						
9:00	7						
9:30	8						
10:00	9						
10:30	10						
11:00	11						
11:30	12						
12:00	13						
12:30	14						
13:00	15						
13:30	16						
14:00	17						
14:30	18						
15:00	19						
15:30	20						
16:00	21						
16:30	22						
17:00	23						
17:30	24						
18:00	25						

Time Compartment Management Graph—Average Smoker
Page 3 of 5 (Continued)

18:30	26
19:00	27
19:30	28
20:00	29
20:30	30
21:00	31
21:30	32
22:00	33

Time Compartment Management Graph—Average Smoker
Page 4 of 5

Time	Time Compartment No. (TC)	Day 19	Day 20	Day 21	Day 22	Day 23	Day 24
6:00	1						
6:30	2						
7:00	3						
7:30	4						
8:00	5						
8:30	6						
9:00	7						
9:30	8						
10:00	9						
10:30	10						
11:00	11						
11:30	12						
12:00	13						
12:30	14						
13:00	15						
13:30	16						
14:00	17						
14:30	18						
15:00	19						
15:30	20						
16:00	21						
16:30	22						
17:00	23						
17:30	24						
18:00	25						

Time Compartment Management Graph—Average Smoker
Page 4 of 5 (Continued)

18:30	26
19:00	27
19:30	28
20:00	29
20:30	30
21:00	31
21:30	32
22:00	33

Time Compartment Management Graph—Average Smoker
Page 5 of 5

Time	Time Compartment No. (TC)	Day 25	Day 26	Day 27	Day 28	Day 28	Day 30
6:00	1						
6:30	2						
7:00	3						
7:30	4						
8:00	5						
8:30	6						
9:00	7						
9:30	8						
10:00	9						
10:30	10						
11:00	11						
11:30	12						
12:00	13						
12:30	14						
13:00	15						
13:30	16						
14:00	17						
14:30	18						
15:00	19						
15:30	20						
16:00	21						
16:30	22						
17:00	23						
17:30	24						
18:00	25						

Time Compartment Management Graph—Average Smoker
Page 5 of 5 (Continued)

18:30	26
19:00	27
19:30	28
20:00	29
20:30	30
21:00	31
21:30	32
22:00	33

Time Compartment Management Graph—Heavy Smoker
Page 1 of 10

Time	Compartment No.	Day 1	Day 2	Day 3	Day 4	Day 5	Day 6
6:00	1						
6:15	2						
6:30	3						
6:45	4						
7:00	5						
7:15	6						
7:30	7						
7:45	8						
8:00	9						
8:15	10						
8:30	11						
8:45	12						
9:00	13						
9:15	14						
9:30	15						
9:45	16						
10:00	17						
10:15	18						
10:30	19						
10:45	20						
11:00	21						
11:15	22						
11:30	23						
11:45	24						
12:00	25						

Time Compartment Management Graph—Heavy Smoker
Page 1 of 10 (Continued)

12:15	26
12:30	27
12:45	28
13:00	29
13:15	30
13:30	31
13:45	32

Time Compartment Management Graph—Heavy Smoker
Page 2 of 10

Time	Compartment No.	Day 1	Day 2	Day 3	Day 4	Day 5	Day 6
14:00	33						
14:15	34						
14:30	35						
14:45	36						
15:00	37						
15:15	38						
15:30	39						
15:45	40						
16:00	41						
16:15	42						
16:30	43						
16:45	44						
17:00	45						
17:15	46						
17:30	47						
17:45	48						
18:00	49						
18:15	50						
18:30	51						
18:45	52						
19:00	53						
19:15	54						
19:30	55						
19:45	56						
20:00	57						

Time Compartment Management Graph—Heavy Smoker
Page 2 of 10 (Continued)

20:15	58
20:30	59
20:45	60
21:00	61
21:15	62
21:30	63
21:45	64
22:00	65

Time Compartment Management Graph—Heavy Smoker
Page 3 of 10

Time	Compartment No.	Day 7	Day 8	Day 9	Day 10	Day 11	Day 12
6:00	1						
6:15	2						
6:30	3						
6:45	4						
7:00	5						
7:15	6						
7:30	7						
7:45	8						
8:00	9						
8:15	10						
8:30	11						
8:45	12						
9:00	13						
9:15	14						
9:30	15						
9:45	16						
10:00	17						
10:15	18						
10:30	19						
10:45	20						
11:00	21						
11:15	22						
11:30	23						
11:45	24						
12:00	25						

Time Compartment Management Graph—Heavy Smoker
Page 3 of 10 (Continued)

12:15	26
12:30	27
12:45	28
13:00	29
13:15	30
13:30	31
13:45	32

Time Compartment Management Graph—Heavy Smoker
Page 4 of 10

Time	Compartment No.	Day 7	Day 8	Day 9	Day 10	Day 11	Day 12
14:00	33						
14:15	34						
14:30	35						
14:45	36						
15:00	37						
15:15	38						
15:30	39						
15:45	40						
16:00	41						
16:15	42						
16:30	43						
16:45	44						
17:00	45						
17:15	46						
17:30	47						
17:45	48						
18:00	49						
18:15	50						
18:30	51						
18:45	52						
19:00	53						
19:15	54						
19:30	55						
19:45	56						
20:00	57						

Time Compartment Management Graph—Heavy Smoker
Page 4 of 10 (Continued)

20:15	58
20:30	59
20:45	60
21:00	61
21:15	62
21:30	63
21:45	64
22:00	65

Time Compartment Management Graph—Heavy Smoker
Page 5 of 10

Time	Compartment No.	Day 13	Day 14	Day 15	Day 16	Day 17	Day 18
6:00	1						
6:15	2						
6:30	3						
6:45	4						
7:00	5						
7:15	6						
7:30	7						
7:45	8						
8:00	9						
8:15	10						
8:30	11						
8:45	12						
9:00	13						
9:15	14						
9:30	15						
9:45	16						
10:00	17						
10:15	18						
10:30	19						
10:45	20						
11:00	21						
11:15	22						
11:30	23						
11:45	24						
12:00	25						

Time Compartment Management Graph—Heavy Smoker
Page 5 of 10 (Continued)

12:15	26
12:30	27
12:45	28
13:00	29
13:15	30
13:30	31
13:45	32

Time Compartment Management Graph—Heavy Smoker
Page 6 of 10

Time	Compartment No.	Day 13	Day 14	Day 15	Day 16	Day 17	Day 18
14:00	33						
14:15	34						
14:30	35						
14:45	36						
15:00	37						
15:15	38						
15:30	39						
15:45	40						
16:00	41						
16:15	42						
16:30	43						
16:45	44						
17:00	45						
17:15	46						
17:30	47						
17:45	48						
18:00	49						
18:15	50						
18:30	51						
18:45	52						
19:00	53						
19:15	54						
19:30	55						
19:45	56						
20:00	57						

Time Compartment Management Graph—Heavy Smoker
Page 6 of 10 (Continued)

20:15	58
20:30	59
20:45	60
21:00	61
21:15	62
21:30	63
21:45	64
22:00	65

Time Compartment Management Graph—Heavy Smoker
Page 7 of 10

Time	Compartment No.	Day 19	Day 20	Day 21	Day 22	Day 23	Day 24
6:00	1						
6:15	2						
6:30	3						
6:45	4						
7:00	5						
7:15	6						
7:30	7						
7:45	8						
8:00	9						
8:15	10						
8:30	11						
8:45	12						
9:00	13						
9:15	14						
9:30	15						
9:45	16						
10:00	17						
10:15	18						
10:30	19						
10:45	20						
11:00	21						
11:15	22						
11:30	23						
11:45	24						
12:00	25						

Time Compartment Management Graph—Heavy Smoker
Page 7 of 10 (Continued)

12:15	26
12:30	27
12:45	28
13:00	29
13:15	30
13:30	31
13:45	32

Time Compartment Management Graph—Heavy Smoker
Page 8 of 10

Time	Compartment No.	Day 19	Day 20	Day 21	Day 22	Day 23	Day 24
14:00	33						
14:15	34						
14:30	35						
14:45	36						
15:00	37						
15:15	38						
15:30	39						
15:45	40						
16:00	41						
16:15	42						
16:30	43						
16:45	44						
17:00	45						
17:15	46						
17:30	47						
17:45	48						
18:00	49						
18:15	50						
18:30	51						
18:45	52						
19:00	53						
19:15	54						
19:30	55						
19:45	56						
20:00	57						

Time Compartment Management Graph—Heavy Smoker
Page 8 of 10 (Continued)

20:15	58
20:30	59
20:45	60
21:00	61
21:15	62
21:30	63
21:45	64
22:00	65

Time Compartment Management Graph—Heavy Smoker
Page 9 of 10

Time	Compartment No.	Day 25	Day 26	Day 27	Day 28	Day 29	Day 30
6:00	1						
6:15	2						
6:30	3						
6:45	4						
7:00	5						
7:15	6						
7:30	7						
7:45	8						
8:00	9						
8:15	10						
8:30	11						
8:45	12						
9:00	13						
9:15	14						
9:30	15						
9:45	16						
10:00	17						
10:15	18						
10:30	19						
10:45	20						
11:00	21						
11:15	22						
11:30	23						
11:45	24						
12:00	25						

Time Compartment Management Graph—Heavy Smoker
Page 9 of 10 (Continued)

12:15	26
12:30	27
12:45	28
13:00	29
13:15	30
13:30	31
13:45	32

Time Compartment Management Graph—Heavy Smoker
Page 10 of 10

Time	Compartment No.	Day 25	Day 26	Day 27	Day 28	Day 29	Day 30
14:00	33						
14:15	34						
14:30	35						
14:45	36						
15:00	37						
15:15	38						
15:30	39						
15:45	40						
16:00	41						
16:15	42						
16:30	43						
16:45	44						
17:00	45						
17:15	46						
17:30	47						
17:45	48						
18:00	49						
18:15	50						
18:30	51						
18:45	52						
19:00	53						
19:15	54						
19:30	55						
19:45	56						
20:00	57						

Time Compartment Management Graph—Heavy Smoker
Page 10 of 10 (Continued)

20:15	58
20:30	59
20:45	60
21:00	61
21:15	62
21:30	63
21:45	64
22:00	65

22

The Final Countdown

Personally speaking

There are many people that want to know how I did it. No matter how many times I tell them it doesn't matter because they still have to find *their own way*, they still want to see my way…so here it is. Again, this is not a definitive guide. This is to simply show you what worked for me. For me they were cumulative so I kept doing ALL the relevant steps until I was smoke free for 4 weeks. Understand that I did these things daily, yes, even when I didn't feel like it. If you use this as a guide, just remember to take what you can use, add some of your own, tailor it for yourself and win this fight for you and your freedom once and for all.

One more thing that really helped me is this: I asked myself over and over through the difficult days, "What's the worst thing that can happen if I don't smoke?" And you know what? I never could honestly come up with a good enough answer to have one. All I kept thinking is I'll be really pissed off all day, and as ludicrous as that is, that's the only thing that made me realize I will not die if I choose not to smoke, so I just chose not to. And the kicker is I know it sounds so ridiculously simple, but why shouldn't it be?

1. Four weeks and counting:

- Write a list of reasons for doing this and keep them in you wallet. Read them twice daily at the bare minimum. Read it in the Costco line, at the gas station and at the supermarket. Find your emotional strength and channel it! Mine was anger.

- Research, read and print out a few motivating articles. My favorite was where the guy was saying that smokers are less intelligent that non-smokers. I made me mad, no it made me insane, and that helped me tremendously.

- Do the sporadic breaking up of your smoke breaks that I explained earlier. Skip one of your smokes each day (regardless of which one) just to prove to yourself that you're not going to die without it. This is a great method to gain confidence.

- Talk to God. Ask Him to help dissolve your fears.

2. One week and counting:

- If you feel you need support, tell your friends and family about your plan. If not then don't. I told no one until day 3…but I kept the 'no turning back' attitude and the commitment to myself. Remember the ATV analogy?

- Internet support groups need committed people like you and I. Join one and post daily because there is strength in unity, even on a cyber level. You may provide just as much support to someone else as they are to you…and that is a beautiful thing as well as spiritually rewarding.

- Figure out when your last smoke will be. Live it in your head. Do positive self-talk. Talk aloud to your subconscious mind, your dashboard, your Coleman grill or your dog. The spoken word is powerful. I used to talk to my Boxer, Chelsea about how I needed to win this fight.

- **Important:** Keep doing the all the things from steps 1 and 2 above that are relevant to you.

3. Four days and counting:

- If you haven't done this yet, buy a small tablet and makes notes on when and why you think you smoke as well as why you're quitting.

- Start thinking and living in you mind, all the time you're going to have when you don't smoke. Go over your benefits list in your wallet in detail.

- Keep doing your homework: Journal entries, posting on websites, research, etc. Knowledge and emotion together can be your catalyst for this undertaking.

- **Important:** Keep doing all the things from the above sections 1 thru 3 that are relevant for you.

4. Three days and counting:

- There are many things you can do with the money you aren't going to be spending on cigarettes. Start making a list of what you'll do with it.

- On your support group, there should be a link to a "quit meter" onto your computer. This is an awesome motivating tool that helps you mark your progress.

- **Important:** Again, keep doing all the things from the above sections 1 thru 4 that apply.

5. Two days and counting:

- Think of who you'd like to reach out to when you need help and get them to agree to "be there" for you. Friends will always do this if you need them. The support group is also always there too.

- **Important:** Not to be redundant, but keep doing all the things from above sections 1 thru 5 that apply.

6. One day and counting:

- The evening before your first day, clean the inside of your car out well. Get an air freshener for it so there's no lingering smoke odor. Keep just enough smokes to get you through the last day; get rid of the rest. All ashtrays must be chucked. Wash the laundry that smells of cigarettes.

- Make a "to-do" list for tomorrow. Make it a long one; you do not want any spare time on that first day. Bust your tail and work up a sweat.

- Go to "www.thetruth.com" and watch a couple commercial clips. If that doesn't get to you, I'm not sure what will.

- **Important:** Keep doing all the things that have worked for you. Keep that emotion on your sleeve.

- *Pray…Pray…Pray.* On this night I prayed like I'd never prayed before. He helped me in ways that cannot be verbalized, just as He will you. Humility is liberating.

7. Day one. You are now a non-smoker:

- Remember; stay busy with your "to-do" list. Do the lawn, wash cars, go bike riding, clean the fireplace, paint a bedroom, fix the leaky faucet, go swimming, wash the windows, clean the garage and a million others things. Then when you're exhausted, go treat yourself to dinner at one of you favorite places. Enjoy the food. Know that you are starting a new way of life. Embrace it, embrace the freedom.

- From here on out it's up to you. What you've learned and studied will help you. Keep that emotional motivation on your sleeve and be able to tap into in on a moments notice.

- If you're comfortable with it, tell people that you know or meet: This is my first day, or second day, or fifth…but let someone know. Don't forget to post on the Internet Support Group daily, numerous times if needed.

- Just remember that when you're craving one, think about how the tobacco companies have contributed to doing this to you. They control you…don't you dare let them win this! It's killing you and they don't give a crap! That just got under my skin like nothing else. If it works for you too, then great! Think of the hundreds reasons there are not to have one. Don't rationalize, just commit and be accountable to yourself.

- Ask yourself this: What is the worst thing that will happen if I don't smoke? The answer is nothing. Then realize that every time you pass a craving, you're one step closer to being totally free. It gets easier with time and also your resolve will get stronger with time.

- Ask yourself: "What the worst thing that can happen if I don't smoke?" If you come up with a valid answer, you'll be the first. Keep it in perspective.

- Do all the things from this book, some of your own creativeness and the above steps to help you stay clean. You can do this. *And don't forget what your knees are for.*

In Closing

Okay so it's going to be tough for a few weeks but so what? Boot camp was tough but I didn't die. Quitting was also tough, but I didn't die there either. You're going to look back and laugh when this is done. My first 3 weeks of being smoke free I was a short-tempered, nasty, uncaring pain in the butt with a foul attitude to my family and everyone around me. But one thing I kept asking myself is, "What's the worst that can happen if I don't have a cigarette?" And you know what? I never came up with an answer worthy of starting again, so I just refused. I told everyone to please just tolerate me and help me through the rough time and they did, just like all of your important supporters will do.

Understand that you will be challenged. Just when you quit, your car might breakdown, or you may get turned down for that promotion you thought was yours, of you'll find out that your Mom's birthday package was lost by the carrier, or a million other things that will test you. Do not even think for a minute that smoking will do anything to resolve issues that arise in your life. Furthermore, it will do nothing more than hurt you both physically, but more so mentally by putting a nail into that coffin that you're now ready to climb out of.

Don't over think this thing either. There are people that want to know every single step, every step to create that step, and the steps to those step creating steps and it's just crazy but in reality, they're just putting off something that's going to be tough. Once you know you're going to quit, just get it done. All your ducks might not be perfectly aligned and that's okay; just get started. There is no substitution for a moral victory of this magnitude, nor is there a shortcut. Get an attitude and get this done, just don't get caught up in that hype, it's useless.

There are few things that give me the feeling of satisfaction that writing does, but one of those few things is helping another human being. I struggled with smoking for so long I had nearly lost all hope that I could ever quit. The Bible says that if we have only the faith of a mustard seed, then we can still move the mountain. Well, I didn't want to move a mountain; I just wanted to quit smoking cigarettes…and I knew that I had at least that much faith left in me. Well, I did finally kick this pig and it's my sincere prayer that if I can help just a handful of people succeed at quitting cigarettes, then this undertaking has been well worth the time and effort.

Now go do what you know you need to do; and don't you dare let them win…

God Bless.

Sincerely,
Christopher A. Chausse

978-0-595-38099-2
0-595-38099-9

Printed in the USA
CPSIA information can be obtained
at www.ICGtesting.com
LVHW040749161124
796811LV00010B/168